Power
Partnering

Power Partnering

A Strategy for Business Excellence in the 21st Century

Sean Gadman

Butterworth-Heinemann
Boston Oxford Johannesburg Melbourne New Delhi Singapore

HD
58.82
G33
1997

Library of Congress Cataloging-in-Publication Data

Gadman, Sean, 1947–
    Power partnering : a strategy for business excellence in the 21st century / Sean Gadman.
       p. cm.
    Includes bibliographical references and index.
    ISBN 0-7506-9809-8 (pbk.)
    1. Organizational learning.   2. Organizational change.
    3. Interorganizational relations.   4. Creative ability in business.
    I. Title
    HD58.82.G33   1997   96–26398
    658.4′06—dc20   CIP

British Library Cataloguing-in-Publication Data
A catalogue record for this book is available from the British Library.

The publisher offers special discounts on bulk orders of this book.
For information, please contact:
Manager of Special Sales
Butterworth–Heinemann
313 Washington Street
Newton, MA 02158–1626
Tel: 617-928-2500
Fax: 617-928-2620
Order number: EY-443E-DP

For information on all Business publications available, contact our World Wide Web home page at: http://www.bh.com/bb

10 9 8 7 6 5 4 3 2 1

Printed in the United States of America

Just as in our daily habits we are affected by new circumstances and by fresh ideas, so are the minds of men influenced by their various life patterns. There are a thousand kinds of men, each differing in desire: Each has his own intent, each burns with a different fire.

Gerald of Wales (1146–1223)

Table of Contents

Foreword

MEMOS TO SEAN
Starting the Conversation
Charles M. Savage

MEMO

To: Sean

From: Charles

Re: The Past: "Fitting in"

Before I write the foreword for your wonderful book, *Power Partnering*, I thought I had better check some ideas.

Your work offers such exciting possibilities for companies and other organizations to rethink the way they work together, that I want to make sure I have appreciated the richness of your thought.

Am I so hopelessly stuck in the "scientific mindset" of the past? This seems strange because Newtonian science helped free people from debilitating superstition. It also enabled our companies to rip open nature and tear out its riches.

The mechanics of science have given us the metaphor of the clock. Regular and orderly. Each part meshes with the other. We have needed many of these machines to indeed free the wealth of nature. But at what price? By hiding our own human nature?

Are you suggesting "clock logic" so dominates our thinking that we feel compelled to fit in, rather than to let our rough and spontaneous edges have their own room? Is there no room for our creativity and innovative talents within the kingdom of the clock?

Charles

MEMO

To: Sean

From: Charles

Date: Tomorrow

Re: The Future: "Outfitting"

If the past is weighted down the the inevitable, does the future not drown in the possible? If there are so many things which could be done, created, and innovated, how do I keep from being overwhelmed? In order to get ready for the future, I or my company can outfit my thinking with all kinds of imaginary possibilities, but how do I choose?

You seem to be suggesting that I start in the future, and work back. This you call "reverse logic." If I or my company has left the comfort of our confinement in the past, might not we be overwhelmed by the options in the future?

Where are our roots? What gives us our stability? From what platform can we spring forth?

Charles

MEMO

To: Sean

From: Charles

Date: Today

Re: The Present: "Misfitting Together"

Maybe I have been too quick in my conclusions. As I think more about what you are saying, I realize you are anchoring us in a present, a present not subject to "either/or" thinking, but one which builds on the richness of "both/and" conversations between diverse individuals and diverse companies, and between the past and future. By "misfitting together," we can build of the richness of our diverse knowledge and visions of yesterday, today, and tomorrow. Indeed, we live in and are nurtured by both the past and the future, and this can become a rich context for meaningful conversations with ourselves, one another, our companies, our suppliers, our customers, and our customers' customers.

There is a spaciousness in this present, because it is inclusive of what we know and have experienced, and yet is open to what we don't know and can create together. The past and the future are misfits, one wants conformity, one wants us to fit in, and the other exudes with possibilities if we are outfitted correctly. They are wonderful misfits, and in this vortex of oughts and coulds, the both/and, we find our freedom to bring the richness of who we are as individuals and companies, of partnering our pasts and futures into a co-creative process.

I just noticed how often you have used verbs instead of nouns. You did not call your book *Power Partners*, but *Power Partnering* instead. You do not talk of vision, but visioning. You do not talk about values, but valuing. Interesting! Are you suggesting the word business is more a verb than a noun? Is this the energy behind power partnering?

Contracts are nouns, conversations are verbs. Do we not find ourselves and our possibilities in conversation and dialogue with another? Certainly Boeing engaged in a serious and systematic conversation with its sub-contractors in the building of the 777. It created the context in which other companies could design their component parts. Steelcase dialogues with its customers in understanding their aspirations for new working environments. Are they not both power partnering through quality dialogue with their suppliers, partners, and customers? Is this not what ABB is doing when it "thinks global and acts local?"

If I understand you correctly, you are suggesting that the platform for the future is based not just on the past, but on our values and ability to value. These give us the stability to be creative together. Is this what you are getting at in your word "stagility," the interplay between the stabilizing power of valuing and the agility of creative thought together?

I think I notice something else very important. Even though you use the "power" reference in terms of "power partnering," you seem really to be talking about relationships which energize. Is this true? Is this not "power with," instead of "power over?" This shift, if I have understood it, is indeed energizing.

Isn't this what the Internet is all about, collaborative dialogue? We are free to move around, explore possibilities, see connections, and follow diverse linkages. We can anchor ourselves in our own creative home page as a basis for building our unique and energizing dialogues with others.

We find energy, because we see and value one another as individuals and companies, and we can appreciate one another's capabilities, and at the same time help one another reach our respective aspirations. This is a much different model from the linear "value chain" which, upon further reflection, is very mechanical and clock like. By beginning with the possibilities of the future, you seem to be broadening the context for meaningful conversations in the present, and further enriched by the past.

I am not sure I fully understand everything you are saying, but somehow I feel energized and look forward to continuing our dialogue of discovery. And I hope that we can broaden this network of conversation.

If you think I have understood your book well enough, I'd be glad to write the foreword. Better still, perhaps our readers are already writing their own forewords, in deeds and not just words, through their skillful power partnering and webs of meaningful conversations. It is exciting and energizing to participate in these broader dialogues. Thanks, Sean, for inspiring us and revealing a most valuable part of our human nature, our ability to remember, dream, and create together.

Charles

Acknowledgments

My childhood heroes, John Lennon and Paul McCartney, wrote "In the end, the love you take/Is equal to the love you make." In keeping with the theme of this book, the end has become the beginning; and, as I write these introductory words as the last stage of completing this book, I have an enormous sense of pride and accomplishment and a deep feeling of love and gratitude for the people who supported me on my journey.

Firstly, I want to offer my sincere thanks to Charles Savage whose guidance and insights shaped my ideas profoundly. His unfailing support contributed enormously to underlying themes expressed in this book. There are many other people, some mentioned in the bibliography and others too numerous to mention here, who have played a significant role in influencing the direction of my life. I thank them all. I am especially grateful to Kelly Breazeale and Ann Cunliffe for their tireless efforts in reading and shaping the manuscript. I deeply appreciate their help and commentary.

I owe a special word of thanks to my editor, Karen Speerstra, whose unquestioning faith in my ability to write infused me with the confidence and commitment to give my best. I am also deeply grateful to the people at Butterworth-Heinemann whose creative genius transformed the manuscript into a book of the highest quality and whose marketing and sales talents presented it to the world. Without this example of power partnering, there would be no book.

While I feel fortunate to be able to thank so many power partners, I count myself extremely fortunate to be a member of the ultimate power partnership, my family. Without their love and support and the creative environment they provided, the task of writing this book would have been overwhelming. There are also those close to my heart who, while being out of sight in England, are never out of my mind. My mother Thea, my father Jack, my sister Linda, and my brother-in-law John are a special force in my life. Above all, my wife Katherine has shown me the true meaning of relationship and the power of love. She is a constant source of inspiration and her presence in my life is reflected in everything I do. So it is to Katherine and our children, Nick, Nic, and Emilie, that I dedicate this book. Without them, my life would be empty and meaningless. My love for them goes deeper than words can express.

Introduction

The changes underway in today's society are everywhere described in superlatives. Charles Savage talks about "the dawning of the knowledge era"; Edward de Bono calls it "the new Renaissance"; Alvin and Heidi Toffler speak of "a new civilization." While the characterizations are many, their message is consistent; we are living in the turbulent early days of a revolution as significant as any in human history—and one that will come to pass in our lifetime.

A new medium of human communications is emerging, one that may prove to surpass all previous revolutions in its impact on our economic and social life. Microcomputers and advanced electronic communication systems are bringing forth a new economy based on the networking of human knowledge. In this knowledge-based economy, enterprises will create wealth by applying knowledge in entirely new and innovative ways. Their success will be determined more in terms of their ability to acquire, generate, distribute, and apply knowledge than in terms of such hard assets as trucks, assembly lines, and inventory.

Companies like Xerox, Johnson and Johnson, ABB, J.C.Penny, and Banc One are fast realizing the competitive advantages to be gained by aligning their intellectual capital with their strategic mission. At Boeing, for example, the outstanding success of the new Boeing 777, one of the largest and most complex aircraft ever built, has been attributed in large part to a new philosophy of "no secrets" and "no rivalry" both within Boeing and between Boeing and its customers and contractors.

MEMO

To: The Reader

From: Sean

Date: July 1st, 1995

Subject: The Strike at Boeing.

Just read in the news that workers at one of Boeing's divisions in Seattle have gone on strike. They are protesting the company's decision to relocate the work to the Far East where labor costs are significantly lower. One worker said he had to crate his own equipment for transporting to the Far East before being asked to leave.

I wonder whether the fine example set by the 777 team will make a difference to situations like this in the future—or whether the bottom line will always win out in the end.

Sean

In many industries today, companies have gone as far as they can to differentiate themselves from competitors, through their products or by lowering prices. Today's challenge is to invent more creative ways of meeting customer needs. "Power Partnering" is a world-class response to this challenge. By creating relationships with your peers, customers, and suppliers that are mutually benefiting, you will discover a source of insight and creativity that will ensure a long-term competitive advantage. The underlying premise connecting these companies is the belief that success comes from organizing and managing in ways that continually leverage the collective creativity and unique talents of all those involved in the enterprise, whether they be company members, suppliers, customers, or the customers' customers. The essence of such relationships is a genuine valuing of one another, and a building of partnership based on shared aspirations, capability, and trust.

This book presents a powerful new framework for executives, managers, and organizational consultants who wish to transform companies into highly responsive and creative power-partnering enterprises. It outlines the challenges of making such transformations and describes ways in which you can creatively partner knowledge and talent in order to increase dramatically your capacity to seize and profit from the untapped reservoir of opportunities existing in your marketplace. In the following pages, you will be challenged to reflect upon your firmly held perceptions and beliefs, and to discover ways of rekindling your innate capacity to bring forth new and creative ideas—a habit of innovation that, in today's complex and fast-changing environment, is a precondition for personal and organizational success and longevity.

The fundamental premise of this book is that, in order for companies to excel in the knowledge-based economy of the twenty-first century, modern managers must shake off their preoccupation with fixing and controlling their environment. It is an invitation to change the habits of a lifetime. The challenge, as Gareth Morgan puts it, is to "infuse the process of organizing with a spirit of imagination that takes us beyond bureaucratic boxes. We need to find creative ways of organizing and managing that allow us to go with the flow, using new images and ideas as a means of creating shared understandings among those seeking to align their activities in organized ways." In short, we must design our organizations in ways that combine standard practices of excellence with more flexible and self-organizing practices fueled by the innovative ideas of their members.

Throughout this book I include memos to the reader, like the previous one about Boeing, that provide an account of my insights and experiences as they occurred during the life of the project. These enlightening and sometimes painful accounts show how any bold undertaking—in my case writing a book—brings forth a world full of celebrations and banana peels just waiting to bring down the unsuspecting adventurer. As I will explain later, what we do in the world is inseparable from our experience of it. Consequently, the words you are now reading and those you will read later have a great deal to do with me and who I am. My current concerns, my aspirations, my background, my mood, all play their part in shaping the book.

Also, as I write this book, so will I become written by it. My perspective will change as I struggle to put my thoughts into words; and as each new word appears, my writing will be shaped accordingly. I will be making choices about which ideas to include and which to leave out. I will be open to some ideas and totally blind to others. In sharing these moments with you, I hope to provide a fuller and more authentic account of the challenges of doing business in the knowledge era. In a world where companies have gone as far as they can to differentiate themselves through their products or through competitive pricing, power partnering offers an innovative way to delight your customers continually—while staying ahead of your competition.

Part 1

The Age of Partnering

The Challenges of the Knowledge Era

THE INCREASING PACE OF CHANGE

Our journey of development from hunter-gathers to farmers took thousands of years to complete, while our move from the farm to the factory took one-hundred and fifty years. Sixty years ago we began to feel the effects of the information age; already, the winds of change are blowing once again. The new wave of change, in Charles Savage's words (1995), is "our ability to tap into the richest vein of wealth in our society, the knowledge of its members. It is our intellectual capital," Savage says:

> our experiences, our learnings, our intuitions, our capabilities, our metaphors, and our talents that are anvils upon which we will shape our ideas into quality products and services. It is not just what we know, tacitly or explicitly, but how we knit together this knowledge. It is *knowledge* and *knowledging* taken together that provide the foundation for our next economy.

With this new era well underway, the indications are that, unlike earlier revolutions that took place across generations, we will feel its full impact within our lifetimes.

Ironically, this accelerating pace of change can be attributed, in large part, to the information age, which made possible moving previously unimaginable amounts of information around the world in seconds. This ability has introduced increasing levels of complexity and ambiguity into our lives; we literally *know* too much. We *know*, for example, that problems take longer to solve and solutions are short-lived. We *know* that the trust we once bestowed upon our leaders and professionals is no longer well-founded. The myth of omnipotence has been exposed for what it is—a myth. We *know* that they are struggling just like we are. In a recent article on the decline of trust in our institutions, Dean Berry writes:

> The social surveys of Yankelovich and Harris paint a picture of long term decline in the trust that American people place in their leaders and institutions. "Trust in Government," Yankelovich concluded, "declined dramatically, from almost 80% in the '50's to about 33% in 1976. More than 80% of (U.S.) voters say they don't trust those in positions of leadership" as much as they did.

> And Harris reported in "The Cynical Americans" (1989), that: "Nowhere has the decline in confidence and the rise in mistrust been more evident than in people's attitudes towards business and its leadership. Confidence in business and business leadership has fallen, from approximately a 70% level in the late '60s to about 15% today. Many fewer people today than eight years ago believe business is doing a good job of investing its money, or provide steady work for employees. Fewer think that business is hiring, developing, or retaining the best management.

Our response to this lack of direction and seemingly over-whelming complexity is to find answers to questions before the questions themselves change. This approach yields short-term solutions that generate nothing more than a whole set of new questions to worry about. Like puppy dogs chasing our tails, our preoccupation with under-standing what our problems are and how they occur blinds us to the even more important question of why they happen in the first place.

Today's problems come from yesterday's solutions and today's solutions will cause tomorrow's problems.

This fact was lost on one of my clients, who had invested millions of dollars in a new "state of the art" manufacturing system to reduce production costs. The new system was so popular that all competitors wanted one, even though they didn't need one. It turned out that not having a new system automatically took you out of the running for building any of the company's new product lines; everyone feared becoming obsolete. But as equipment costs began to skyrocket, concerned engineers produced forecasts showing that the company would need no more than three high-tech lines to meet projected demands for new products. Their warnings were ignored; it was not long before the market began to soften and demand for the company's products declined to such an extent that they were caught off guard with millions of dollars of excess capacity. Manufacturing facilities around the world were closed down and thousands of people lost their jobs. What began as a creative idea to reduce costs ended as a costly failure.

Gregory Bateson called this phenomenon "the double bind," where solving a problem at one contextual level automatically creates a problem at a more encompassing contextual level, thereby undermining the original solution. We are caught in these endless "double binds," trading one set of problems for another using thinking habits that are simply not up to the challenge of breaking free from our existing thought patterns— patterns of decision-making that are hopelessly inadequate because they are based on outdated assumptions about the way the world works.

These assumptions picture the world as a well-oiled clock-work machine, whose outputs and behaviors can be reduced to predictable equations and quantifiable relationships. Unfortunately, this "clock logic" can't explain the dramatic setbacks experienced by some of the world's most successful companies. Nor can it provide an adequate response to the

MEMO

To: The Reader

From: Sean

Date: October 22nd, 1995

Subject: Sierra Club Fighting to Save America's Environment

Just received a mailing from the Sierra Club asking me to sign a citizen's petition to the president of the United States of America. Among other things, the letter warns of anti-environmental forces in Congress "escalating their all out war on America's environment." Some of the biggest threats, the letter says, are coming from our own Congress:

"Newt Gingrich, Georgia, the Speaker of the House, who is leading the battle to weaken or eliminate our most critical environmental laws and protections.

"Don Young, Alaska, with a 1994 environmental voting record of 0%, chairs the House Resources Committee, which is the central authority over environmental legislation. As chairman, Young vows to gut the Endangered Species Act and block all future wilderness bills.

"Frank Murkowski, Alaska, chairs the Senate Energy and Natural Resources Committee. A staunch anti-environmentalist, he crusaded against almost every land-protection bill that came before this committee and has pledged to open the Arctic National Wildlife Refuge to oil drilling and exploration."

Sean

shocking changes we are presently experiencing in our global political landscape. We have unprecedented stresses on our physical environment—the ozone hole, the greenhouse effect, the pollution of the oceans, the destruction of forest and field. We have big business interests extending their search for natural resources into our wilderness, and environmental laws blocked by politicians who are financed by those big business interests.

While there can be no doubt that science has made outstanding advances in every walk of life, this progress has not been without consequences. As Peter Senge and Fred Kofman (1995) point out:

> The very same skills of separation, analysis, and control that gave us the power to shape our environment are producing ecological and social crisis in our outer world and psychological and spiritual crises in our inner world. Both these crises grow out of our success in separating ourselves from the larger fabric of life. When we begin to understand the origins of our problems, we begin to see that the "existential crisis" of early twentieth-century philosophy and the "environmental crisis" of the late twentieth-century ecology are inseparable—caused by the co-evolution of fragmentary worldviews, social structures, lifestyles, and technology.

With the lightning-fast demands of our stormy and unforgiving business environment producing overwhelming levels of complexity and ambiguity in our lives, why do we still insist on using "clock logic" to figure things out? Why are we still so invested in a mode of thinking that is constantly proving itself to be woefully inadequate for tackling the challenges of this new world order? Clearly, the roots run deep. The legacy of "clock logic" is still very strong.

2

The Legacy of Clock Logic

"Clock logic" emerged in the first half of the nineteenth century as a consequence of the rise of science and technology and as a social movement aimed at applying the achievements of science and technology to the well being of humankind. It is based upon Plato and Aristotle's premise that the objective world of physical reality could be separated from the subjective mental world of an individual's thoughts and feelings—that reality is experienced as independent of the consciousness of the person who interacts with it.

As clock logic gained dominance, so did the idea that human progress could be achieved by harnessing science to create a technology for human ends. It was characterized by three principal doctrines. First, there was a conviction that empirical science was not just a form of knowledge, but the *only* positive source of knowledge in the world. Argument, backed up by hard scientific data, became the means of establishing truth and the basis of an adversarial system in science, law, and politics. Second, there was an intention to cleanse the human mind of mysticism, superstition, and other forms of pseudo-knowledge. Finally, there was a movement to extend scientific knowledge and technical control into human society, such that propositions that were neither analytically or empirically tested were considered meaningless and dismissed as emotive utterances, poetry, or mere nonsense.

This movement lodged most firmly in our institutions of higher education where, today, its artifacts abound. For instance, visitors to Harvard University in Cambridge will see proudly displayed on its gates, letter heads, publications, T-shirts, and ice-hockey pucks the motto "Veritas." This obsessive search for truth remains the hallmark of our universities, colleges, and business schools. They are not so much devoted to the production and distribution of fundamental knowledge in general as they are to furthering a view of knowledge that fosters selective inattention to anything that cannot be supported by hard data. As I write, I am reminded of my first exposure to the passionate and apparently irreconcilable academic debate concerning the ontological and epistemological issues about what constitutes reality. The following is an example of one such debate:

MEMO

To: The Reader
From: Sean
Date: August 21st, 1995
Subject: The Impact of Leadership Conference.

The following letter from Henry Mintzberg, professor of management at McGill University in Montreal, to David Campbell, H. Smith Richardson Senior Fellow at the Center for Creative Leadership in North Carolina, reminds me of how contentious the issue of what constitutes "the Truth" is.

Dear David,

You may be interested in an experience I just had. Near the end of a wonderful conference in Cambridge on "Leadership and Strategic Change," full of nuanced papers and rich discussion, your call for papers for your forthcoming conference on "The Impact of Leadership" appeared. Someone made an overhead of it and when he read out your point number 2: "The study(s) must be data-based—i.e., no conceptual papers, nor anecdotes, nor testimonials unless accompanied by quantifiable data"—well, I'll let you guess the reaction. At Cambridge, we had plenty of concepts and anecdotes, a few superb testimonials and all kinds of data, much of the best of it not quantitative. I suggest you change the name of your conference to "The Lack of Impact of Leadership Research," for that is the overwhelming conclusion to come out of eighty years of exactly the kind of research you call for.

So the Center has caught the American disease. Too bad. You might consider shortening its name by one word.

Sincerely,

Henry Mintzberg

Mintzberg later declined an invitation, by Campbell, to join the conference because, as he put it:

Life is too short. I did this once at one of the Southern Illinois conferences; I diatribed, said what I felt, everyone else got insulted or just yawned and the world continued as it had.

Sean

This story not only highlights the issues surrounding questions concerning the nature of truth; more importantly, it points to the futility of debating the rightness of one position over the other. Debates about who is right and who is wrong inevitably lead to polarization that freezes us in opposition to one another. From our polarized positions, there can be no bridge-building—just more bricks in the wall. "I'm right/You're wrong" can be immensely useful when we are prepared to defer our differences long enough to allow new insights to occur as a direct consequence of those differences. As the late Nobel prize-winning physicist Richard Feynman said:

> I can live with doubt and uncertainty and not knowing. I think it is more interesting to live not knowing than to have answers which might be wrong. I have approximate answers and possible beliefs and different degrees of certainty about different things, but I am not absolutely sure about anything and there are many things I don't know anything about.

In our Western culture, our loathing for ambiguity has given way to a craving for truth and certainty that is without precedent. This craving has become so natural it no longer occurs to us that there might be other ways; like Einstein said, "what would a fish know about water?" Over the years we have become "wired" for argument and logic, supplemented by heavy doses of statistics and scientific data, to search for and impose "absolute truths" upon one another. We have titles like *How to Argue and Win Every Time* making number one on the *New York Times Book Review*'s list of best-sellers. We have Stephen Covey's *The Seven Habits of Highly Effective People* and Deepak Chopra's *The Seven Spiritual Laws of Success*, not to mention Fisher and Ury's *Getting to Yes: Negotiating Agreement Without Giving In*.

I recently became involved in a dialogue aimed at surfacing these issues and gaining a deeper understanding of the consequences of this type of thinking. The following memo relates the opening dialogue, which sparked so much interest that it seems likely it will endure.

MEMO

To: The Reader

From: Sean

Date: January 10th, 1996

Subject: My Recent Letter to the Editor of
Freedom at Work

Dear Patti,

I read with interest your recent article on "Human Dynamics" (Freedom at Work, December 1995) and was struck by the notion that Freedom at Work *has caught the Industrial Era disease. I worry when I read that "Human Dynamics" has been researched and rigorously documented since 1979. Does that mean that we are all figured out? Can we, should we, generalize and say that each of us fits into one of five distinct dynamics? Do we know, or even care about, the nature of the observer and the perspective she or he is speaking out of?*

Is it possible, or even ethical, to characterize people as a given dynamic while at the same time telling them that we value them? With some people, labels have a nasty habit of sticking and I believe that we are speaking irresponsibly when we subsume entire groups of people into categories.

The temptation to create typologies like Human Dynamics and Meyers-Briggs assumes there are generalizable categories existing outside of the perceptual framework of the observer. I think this is a dangerous assumption and one that is at odds with the transformative power of contextualism, which challenges us to acknowledge that we can never know anything outside of its context.

Sincerely,
Sean Gadman
Teknowledging, Inc.
Newburyport, MA

Response

Dr. Gadman points out a crucial distinction in the use of frameworks to augment our understanding of human processes. In fact, the creators of "Human Dynamics" resist efforts to categorize their work as a typology. They see the ultimate purpose of their work as fostering understanding of how differences in each of us can contribute to greater synergy by complementing one another's processes and dynamics. They encourage the use of the Human Dynamics framework as a way of identifying ones own processes in order to transcend them by integrating others. If the article implied in any way that the use of Human Dynamics is designed to pigeonhole or manipulate people, I sincerely regret the inference. Understanding his comments on this particular concern, Sean is reminding me of *Freedom at Work's* roots in the contextual world view and the discipline of responsible speaking and listening. So am I a lapsed contextualist or merely undisciplined? If I were a disciplined contextualist, how might I have written the article on Human Dynamics? (If I were completely lapsed, I would not be enjoying this issue so much).

Rather than keep this inquiry to myself, I choose to create an opening for dialogue. I've spoken with Dr. Gadman and he and I invite responses to either of the key questions he has raised:

1. Is it dangerous to use frameworks like Human Dynamics or personality typologies to instrument our path in the world?

2. What would you see more (or less) of in *Freedom at Work* if it had a more thoroughly contextual agenda?

Sean

Our intolerance for ambiguity has created a vast market for writers, doctors, futurists, scientists, psychologists, psychotherapists, and the many other "ists" too numerous to mention here, who claim they have figured out ways to remove the ambiguity from our lives. For instance, we have personality frameworks like the "Myers-Briggs Type Indicator," the "Enneagram," and Sandra Seagal's "Human Dynamics," each characterizing distinct and generalizable personality types. These frameworks and many more like them share at least one thing in common; they subsume entire cultures into neatly packaged categories, trademark those categories, and then make lots of money selling them to people who require categories to make their lives as simple as possible. They are so appealing because they provide "silver bullets" that remove all traces of ambiguity from our lives.

I share Gregory Bateson's skepticism (1972) that "we social scientists would do well to hold back our eagerness to control that world which we so imperfectly understand. A screwdriver is not seriously affected when we use it as a wedge and a hammer's outlook on life is not affected because we sometimes use its handle as a simple lever. But in social manipulation our tools are people and people learn and they acquire habits which are more subtle and pervasive than the tricks the blueprinter teaches them." I have grave doubts about the effectiveness and ethics of these practices because, ultimately, they aren't very practical. Life is too complex and effective action is too contextual.

The appeal of this illusion of certainty is woven into the very fabric of our society, from education, health care and politics to government and business. With few exceptions, these institutions have been founded on a clock logic of certainty, predictability, and control. We deal with complexity by "shaking it apart" (the word "analysis" comes from the Greek *ana-*, "throughout," and *lyein*, "to loosen"), studying the pieces and then synthesizing them back into the whole. Likewise, in our institutions, we reduce phenomena to manageable pieces in order to understand and control each piece. We do this by appointing people to control these pieces, and appointing even more people to control the people who control the pieces, and so on. Clock logic has given rise to clock work, and our "clock workplaces" have become, in Charles Savage's words, "cultures of devaluing and distrust," where we:

> continually look for weaknesses and faults in others. We distrust our managers, our colleagues, our suppliers, our competitors, and our customers. In essence, we have designed our institutions to minimize incompetence and deviousness and we pay dearly for this mindset. It impedes the flow of information. It stifles intuition and creativity. It blinds us to new possibilities. It makes our task twice as hard. It adds unbelievable stress to our work and brittleness to our organizations. It brings unnecessary cost to our products and services and makes us less competitive.

Fragmentation, competition, and reactiveness are, according to Peter Senge and Fred Kofman, deeply rooted dysfunctions; and our response, seeking to overcome them, is part of the very mindset that generated them. They are not problems to be solved, Senge and Kofman argue; rather, they are frozen patterns of thought to be dissolved. With the world poised on the threshold of an era of unprecedented complexity and change, it is becoming increasingly clear that we need an alternative to clock logic and clock work—a new way of thinking, feeling, and being. But how can this be achieved? How can we encourage new organizational designs and develop ways of thinking and styles of managing that differentiate us from our competitors by dynamically partnering knowledge to seize tomorrow's rich patterns of highly profitable opportunities?

MEMO

To: The Reader

From: Sean

Date: February 16th, 1996

Subject: An Insightful Response to My Letter to the Editor of *Freedom at Work*

What follows is a response to my letter to the editor of *Freedom at Work*. While I found this response enlightening, I could not see how Human Dynamics was in any way different from the many typologies in existence today. I have included part of Chris's response because of her insightful comment in the last paragraph, which I emphasize here. I feel her remarks capture the essence of power partnering— the motivation to love and the intention to join.

Dear Patti and Sean,

We live in a predominantly mechanistic world, our reductionist views ingrained in us by over three hundred years of Cartesian thinking. In such a world, where we most often conclude that everything is either/or, I would answer your question about typologies with: Yes, indeed it is extremely dangerous! If the typology tells me how you and I are different and omits to also show me how you and I are the same, if we are given a label with no context in which to see ourselves and others, we may then be even further divided.

But what if we lived in a different world? What if there were a way, a more balanced way? As an engineer and a continually learning systems thinker, I have long searched for ways to examine pieces while remembering that they have relationships with each other and to the whole. I have worked hard to live in awareness that the spaces between things are at least as important as the things themselves. What if there were a way of knowing both *the distinctions* and *the oneness in all of us....*

I think I have said enough. It is not my intention to "sell" Human Dynamics. It speaks for itself when experienced. I write simply to offer the possibility of the value of some form of categorization with context. Human Dynamics too can be used for great good or for great destruction. Ultimately, therefore, the answer to your question, dear Patti and Sean, is yes and no! It all comes back to the intent of the user. Is it to join or to divide? Is the fundamental motivation love or is it fear? If our true intention is to join, if we genuinely wish to understand, to appreciate, and to nurture each other and if we're willing to persevere, to choose for understanding again and again—then perhaps anything will work.

Sean

We must move beyond clock logic to infuse the process of organizing and managing with the spirit of insight and innovation, which can take us beyond traditional clockwork structures of devaluing and distrust. We must fashion structures that reflect our fundamental motivation to love—structures that reflect our true intention to join, to understand, and to appreciate. In short, we need nothing less than a totally fresh way of thinking about designing and managing our organizations. We must move beyond clock logic to a way of thinking that frees us from the bounds of reductionism and opens our hearts and minds to the power of partnership. The power of partnership is the power to make the unimaginable possible because we declare it to be so; it is the power to innovate through collective thinking and acting. It is nothing less than the power to invent a future that would not other-wise happen.

Moving Beyond Clock Logic

3

TIME FOR A NEW LOGIC

Einstein said that everything had changed except our way of thinking. Certainly if we are to make progress in our relationships with ourselves and others, we must change our traditional ways of thinking—we must make the shift from "clock logic" to "reverse logic." I call it reverse logic because it is a way of reasoning that avoids being certain about anything, especially why people are the way they are or why they do the things they do. Reverse logic changes the perceptions, emotions, and beliefs of both ourselves and other people through adopting alternatives to argument based on reason and logic. Using reverse logic requires that we quit deluding ourselves with the idea that, if only people would "see reason," or fit into our belief systems, the world would be a better place.

Anthony Blake once characterized the human journey as one that takes us from innocence to experience to higher innocence. Reverse logic recognizes that our challenge is not to seek absolute proof of truth but to attain mastery in reaching increasingly higher levels of innocence. It requires that we understand and explain the complexities of human nature through means other than reason and argument—through a logic that, as Umberto Maturana and Francisco Varela point out, "is rooted in our history where our perceptions are formed and where there is no absolute certainty of truth because our perceptions are blind to the perceptions of others and can only be transcended in a world created with those others." Seeking truth through argument, logic, and reason inevitably leads to negativity, indifference, and attack; the result of such thinking can only be one winner and greater entanglement in "double binds." We only have to reflect upon the many conflicts taking place around the world to understand that, in any war, both sides have truth on their side—a truth that serves their perceptions, a truth that sets up a pattern of blaming and counter blaming, a truth that ensures an even wider division and a continuation and escalation of conflict.

We also know that no matter how long we engage in conflict, there comes a time when, as Abba Eban said, "people of nations behave wisely, once they have exhausted other alternatives." We behave wisely when we realize that winning at someone else's expense doesn't work, or when we simply grow tired of expending the energy necessary to hate and kill people. Whatever the reason for our wisdom, the fact remains that if we truly desire a lasting resolution to our conflicts, we must use reverse logic to create the space and set aside the time to share and mutually value one another's perspectives.

This act of valuing is essential to the innovating process and is fundamental in power partnering relationships. From a power partnering perspective, valuing someone means you pay attention to them as a real person existing out there in the real world—and, more importantly, as reflections of your *inner world* as you see yourself mirrored in them. Likewise, by viewing your business environment as valuable (rather than a threat to be controlled), you see it as a real entity existing out there, and also as a reflection of your inner world mirrored

MEMO

To: The Reader

From: Sean

Date: September 6th, 1995

Subject: Meeting with Martin McGuiness

This morning I met with Martin McGuiness, the chief negotiator and key architect of Sinn Fein's strategy for a lasting peace in Northern Ireland. He told me his people were ready for peace because, "no matter how long we wait, there can only be one resolution to the conflict and that is for all parties to come to the negotiating table."

Shortly after our conversation, the *Boston Herald* ran an article entitled "Unionist Leader Takes Hard Line." In it, the leader of Northern Ireland's largest unionist party, David Trimble, said, "it would be impossible for me to have face-to-face negotiations with Sinn Fein lead negotiator Martin McGuiness because he [McGuiness] has too much blood on his hands. We know he is personally responsible for over a score of murders, he personally pulled the trigger on people." The accusations didn't stop there. In Britain, the *Daily Mail* ran a series of articles condemning Sinn Fein and applauding the British Prime Minister's decision to refuse to talk peace until the IRA hands over its weapons—a demand which, Sinn Fein claims, is without precedent in any other peace process undertaken so far. With so many conflicting perceptions of the truth and so much blaming, the road to peace will be a long and bumpy one and one which clearly will require a new way of thinking if the outcomes are to be different from all previous ones which have failed to resolve the conflict.

Sean

MEMO

To: The Reader

From: Sean

Date: February 14th, 1996

Subject: Cease-fire Violations in the North of Ireland

I was saddened to learn today that violence has, once again erupted in the North. People aren't sure if it's just a remote incident or a more serious prelude to the full-scale resumption of hostilities. As usual, everyone is blaming everyone else for the cause. I wonder what it will take for people to realize the futility of blaming and begin the search for an entirely new approach?

Sean

in it. This point is lost on many companies who encounter great problems when they don't regard their environment in this way. Such companies are still locked in clock logic, seeing themselves as discrete entities surviving against the vagaries of their marketplace—which they mostly regard as a threat. They completely miss the point that the outside world simply cannot be understood in this way.

Tom Clancy's book *The Hunt for Red October* offers a helpful analogy. Attack submarines, like the Red October of Clancy's story, are designed to operate in their environment as quietly and as blindly as possible. They rely on passive sonar and acoustical receptors to detect hostile vessels. Once a target is located, its nationality can be identified by its particular noise, or acoustical signature, which varies with each class of ship. Navigating underwater without sonar is often accomplished with the aid of a complex inertial-navigation system that provides information on a submarine's location based on gravity, the earth's rotation, and the submarine's speed and direction. This information is, in turn, correlated with detailed underwater maps outlining the characteristics of the sea bottom in the area. In newer vessels, analog pictures of the seabed based on previous ocean surveys can be constructed for submarine navigators, giving them a television-like picture of the "ground" in front of them.

A casual observer, snorkeling above an attack submarine, would see none of this. They might describe its movements through the water by saying things like, "it passed through the reef with incredible dexterity by moving its rudder to the left and right"; but this would say nothing about the complex patterns of interactions that make up the inner world of the submarine and the outer world with which it interacts and through which it exists. As Maturana and Varela point out, the idea that systems, whether living or, like the submarine, mechanical, are open to their environment is the product of an attempt to make sense of such systems from the standpoint of an impartial external observer. As such, it does not take into account the perspectives, assumptions, values, and frames of reference of that observer and the fact that all knowing is the product of her or his interpretive process.

This is clock logic at its best—organizational snorkelers, making sense of their environment by imposing their own perspective on it and deluding themselves with the notion that they have got it all figured out. Operating on the basis of such an approach involves a dangerous assumption; as watch companies learned to their detriment in the late 1970s, holding fast to their identity as watchmakers blinded them to the reality of digital and microprocessing technology. When these technologies began to exert a presence in timekeeping products, watch-making companies simply didn't know what hit them until it was too late. When you are a watchmaker everything looks like a watch; if it doesn't, it simply doesn't exist. It has no value, and thus poses no threat. This is a fatal trap many companies are finding themselves caught in today. By taking a wait-and-see approach to their future they miss the important opportunities that occur when they intentionally set out to invent their future—a future that would not otherwise happen.

REVERSE LOGIC

To understand why marketplaces and people do the things they do, we must go beyond clock logic to take on a view of the world that is anything but clockwork. I call this way of reasoning reverse logic, a view of the world in which there can be no proof of truth outside of our perceptions and the strong belief systems they form. Reverse logic yields a world with no fixed point of view to which we can anchor ourselves in order to affirm and defend our position. Reverse logic acknowledges that the world we create is both a reflection of our inner patterns of perception and our relationship to the outer world. Whether experiencing submarines, marketplaces, or people, we are essentially doing the same thing; yet, while we would never presume to know the inner and outer worlds of submarines (unless we have considerable expertise in that domain), we would not exercise the same degree of caution when it comes to describing and interpreting our business environment and the people that are an essential part of its makeup. It could be argued that people are infinitely more complex than submarines.

Moving beyond this kind of clock logic requires a radically different approach to business—the power partnering approach. Power partnering is founded on reverse logic, requires a continual questioning and knowing of your suppliers, customers, customer's customers, competition, and yourself as a seamless process. In a power partnership you recognize and accept both that you are a reflection of your market environment, and that your market environment is a reflection of yourself. There is no separation, no fixed point of reference to which you can anchor your knowing and defend its validity. Once freed from that illusion, you free yourself to create your environment, your future and your identity at the same time.

This self-referencing process is analogous to looking through a window at the world outside while, at the same time, observing your reflection in the glass. You constantly compare the two images to determine how closely they match. If there is darkness outside then you refer to the clearer self image reflected inside, provided there is sufficient internal illumination. Likewise, if there is too much illumination outside—brought on by our passion for certainty—then you don't see your reflection in the glass at all. In other words, if you want to understand your environment you must first begin by understanding yourself, because your understanding of your environment is always a projection of who you are. This is the characteristic nature of power partnerships; they exist as self-referencing systems maintaining a strong connection and inseparability between who they are and how the world appears to them.

You may have heard the story of the motorist who narrowly escaped a head-on collision with another car. As the offending vehicle passed by, its owner yelled out, "Pig!"—to which the motorist indignantly responded, "Idiot!" Seconds later, as he rounded a sharp bend in the road, he ran into a pig and wrecked his car. The triggered pattern sets off emotions and stereotypes that directly affect our perception of what is in front of us. This changed perception determines what we pay attention to and what patterns we use. The result is that we really do experience something that is different from what another person might experience. The phenomenon of triggering and reconstruction is natural behavior in any patterning system. On the whole it is immensely useful; life would be impossible without it. Nevertheless, triggering is one of the factors that ensures that there can be no truth in perception. What we experience is based on *our perception of what is there* rather than *what is actually there.*

Without this patterning capacity every human activity—even getting dressed in the morning—would take an unacceptable amount of time. Consider the millions of people who drive along roads every day using patterns of perception and reaction and only occasionally having to work things out. Or consider the airplane mishap in Sioux City, Iowa, in which the captain avoided a considerably greater loss of life than did occur by flying his stricken plane to a nearby airport and crash landing it. Later, when he attempted to explain how he had flown his aircraft with no hydraulic power, it became clear to experts that he had performed the impossible. No flight simulator had been programmed for such an eventuality; it was only through reflection after the fact that an explanation of how the plane and the captain did what they did could be constructed.

There are routine patterns of perception, which are the means by which we can recognize knives, forks, and people. There are routine patterns of meaning, which are the means by which we can listen, read, and communicate. We are guided by these patterns; at the same time, we are their creators in an ongoing process. It is not possible to pause reflect and make conscious choices for every event flowing by in our stream of consciousness. Instead, we routinely monitor our environment and respond in terms of internal patterns that are triggered reflexively in the course of our interaction with it. Often, this process breaks down when we are confronted with entirely new situations that trigger inappropriate responses, as the following memo demonstrates.

MEMO

To: The Reader
From: Sean
Date: February 1st, 1996
Subject: Rattlesnake Eggs

While visiting a gift shop in Colorado, my attention was drawn to a novelty item that was for sale. It was an envelope with a picture of a diamond-back rattlesnake poised to strike. Beneath the picture was written "Rattlesnake Eggs," followed by a warning sign in red letters: "To avoid incubation keep in a cool place." As I opened the envelope, I unknowingly released a pre-loaded device hidden inside that produced a rattling sensation in my hand—whereupon I instantly dropped the package and leaped backwards into a crowd of shoppers.

I decided to conduct an experiment to see if I could replicate the phenomenon and sent my parents a packet of the "Rattlesnake Eggs." Nothing happened for months, and I thought my experiment had failed. Then, sure enough, a few months later my father called telling me he had misplaced my gift and while spring cleaning, my mother had found and opened it. My experiment was a total success. Both I and my mother had enough evidence of the damaging effects of rattlesnake bites to know what to do if we ever

---

encountered a rattlesnake. The pattern was formed in our minds; all it took was a picture, an envelope, and a pre-loaded gizmo to trigger our response. The strength of my belief system created a perception that simply was the truth—not an absolute truth but one shaped by, amongst other things, my values, assumptions, world views, interests, and perceptions. If I had sent the same packet to an expert on poisonous reptiles, her or his response might well have been different.

Sean

So how have your perceptions been shaped? What are the factors that bring meaning to your world? Are you aware of your routine patterns of perception and are they relevant to the present and future challenges you face in your business? Your organization's self-image is a critical element in shaping almost every aspect of its functioning. Consequently, you would be well advised to spend some time discovering what it is, and ensuring that you have an appropriate sense of identity. In the next chapter we will take a look at some of the key factors that shape logic and how each, it its own way, is both influenced by its context and cannot be understood outside of that context.

4

Factors that Shape Logic

Logic is the art of reasoning. It is the skillful manipulation of the perceptual networks of interlinked patterns that make up our inner world; and it is these inner pathways that shape our response to the outer world. While there can be no doubt we are experiencing a real world, a closer look tells us we cannot separate our perception of that world "out there" from how it appears to us "in here." From a patterning perspective, our environment is both an integral part of us and a reflection of who we are. In the act of living we exist in an environment that is of our own creation. This inseparability cannot be picked apart and studied independently of the entire system. To do so would be to change the entire reasoning of that system. Here are five key factors that I believe are instrumental in shaping our logic:

1. Logic and History
2. Logic and Intention
3. Logic and Mood
4. Logic and Language
5. Logic and Context

LOGIC AND HISTORY

Knowledge is always the result of interpretation—which in turn depends, as Fernando Flores and Terry Winograd point out, on the entire previous history of the interpreter. Our self-concept and corresponding world view, our entire experience of experiencing, is the result of our biological and social history. Consequently, there is much in life, such as skin color, body shape, gender, and mental and physical ability, that is inevitable and determined. However, having said this, it is important to remember that there is much that is possible even with these constraints. For instance, I may not be biologically designed to run a mile in under four minutes; yet I can, with the right attitude and physical conditioning, compete in next year's Boston marathon.

The challenge we face every day of our lives is discerning the difference between *inevitability* and *possibility*. Put another way, it is the challenge of maintaining the fine balance between making things happen and letting them happen. For instance, if I had listened to some people in my life, I would never have achieved the things I have achieved. On the other hand, if I had listened to others, I would not have experienced some of the hardships I have experienced. It's a tough call. Maturana and Varela liken this balancing act to:

"walking on the razor's edge." In their view, we must seek a *via media* to understand the regularity of the world we are experiencing at every moment, but without any point of reference independent of ourselves that would give certainty to our descriptions and cognitive assertions. Indeed, the whole mechanism of generating ourselves as describers and observers tells us that our world, as the world which we bring forth with others, will always have precisely that mixture of regularity and mutability, that combination of solidity and shifting sand, so typical of human experience when we look at it up close.

All too often we convince ourselves that something is unattainable, only to find that someone else, just like us, did it. I never cease to be amazed at the number of people in

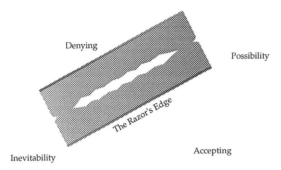

Figure 4-1

organizations who blame "management" for their ill fortune. They unthinkingly place their destiny in the hands of someone else. Whether it be in organizations or elsewhere, your ability to maximize your potential is directly related to where you place the razor's edge. Placing your destiny largely in the hands of someone else may seem to involve little risk, but it imposes serious constraints on your ability to grow. In contrast, believing yourself to be in control of your destiny opens up the possibility for significant growth and involves significant risk.

Where we place the razor's edge depends to a large extent upon our personal history. Some people I have talked to believe their predisposition to life's challenges is due to traumatic experiences early in life; others attribute their attitude to family background. The degree to which we perceive our reality to be internally or externally focused depends on events that occur over a long period of time and involve continual exposure or very important events that occur over a relatively short period of time. For instance, having made the terrible decision to place her brain-damaged son into the permanent care of an institution, one young CEO told me, "when I took my first step out of that place, I decided never to waste another moment of my life." Ultimately, where we place the razor's edge is a matter of personal choice and how we choose is a matter of history. If we say we can, we are right; if we say we can't, we are right. It really depends on the degree of choice we give ourselves—how much we listen to others, and how much we listen to ourselves.

LOGIC AND INTENTION

Back in fifteenth-century England, three stonemasons were asked what they were doing. One said he was chiseling granite; the second said he was carving blocks of stone into cubes; and the third said he was building a cathedral. As self-referencing systems, the world we create is a direct consequence of our purposeful being in that world. If something is not important to us, we can be looking straight at it and never see it. The point is made in an oft-quoted aphorism: "All attention is intention, and all intention is attention." In other words, like the stonemasons, what we say we are up to in life has the effect of directing our attention in a special way. We do not see what we do not see, and what we do not see does not exist.

The following true story may help illustrate this point. When we first moved into our cottage on the shores of Galway Bay, I could never understand why, when I pulled my small sailing dingy down to the water's edge, it would fall off the trailer at one particular spot. I was convinced there was something wrong with either the driveway, the trailer, or both, and went to great lengths to correct the problem. Some days it wouldn't happen, other days it would. There was simply no logical explanation for why my dingy fell off its trailer. Then one day, my neighbor happened to be out when I was putting my boat in the water and it again fell off its trailer. He said, "I think I know what your problem is." "What would a farmer know about sailing?" I thought. "All right John," I said indignantly, "enlighten me."

"It's your mast," he said. "Its getting caught up in the power cable between your cottage and Michael's cottage next door. When its cold, you won't have a problem, because the cable will tighten and your mast passes underneath. When its hot, the cable sags and it catches the top of your mast. I have to watch for cables all the time when I drive my tractor around the village. That's how I saw it; I knew where to look."

My neighbor knew where to look because in fulfilling his purpose as a farmer, he had to be watchful when moving his farming equipment around the village in safety. Without intending to be a farmer, there would be no farm, no tractor, no combined harvester, no crops, no sheep, no cattle, no power cables. No purpose, no meaning. Everything that exists has a certain power of self-determination, or selective actualization. The power is possible, because the whole of existence is self determined. We are some kind of possibility making our future different from our past. This is one key definition of intention, that your future will not be the same as your past. When John Lennon wrote "Imagine," he said he was inspired by the concept of positive prayer: "If you want to get a car, get the car keys. Get it? 'Imagine' is saying that if you can imagine, a world appears."

LOGIC AND MOOD

Have you ever searched high and low for the pencil you placed behind your right ear, or rifled through the mountain of papers on your desk looking for the spectacles that are perched on top of your head? So it is with mood; you know it's there, but you just can't put your finger on it. Moods such as denial, resentment, resignation, anxiety, depression, peace, and ambition have one thing in common: they bring meaning to our lives. Yet, as I have said throughout this book, their presence is contextual, being both real and imagined by us. For instance, provided the sky is clear, there will be a sunset this evening; more than likely, there will be one tomorrow evening, and hopefully for many more evenings to come. However, the sunset I experience as I sit relaxing on a terrace with a glass of wine in front of me after a perfect game of golf will be quite different from the one I experience as I watch the ferry I should have been sailing on disappear into the sunset because I arrived at the dockside too late. In the first case, I will be experiencing the sunset from a mood of peace; in the second case, from a mood of anger and frustration because my car broke down causing me to miss the boat.

Much of the meaning we bring to our lives is influenced by our mood. For instance, there are many people who are resigned to the idea that we are who we are, and there is not a lot we can do about it. Alternatively, there are some who feel hopeful that, while there is much in life that appears inevitable, we do have some degree of choice about who we are and how we intend to live our lives. Essentially, our moods are a consequence of our predisposition to both who we say we are and who we really are. We must constantly choose between making things happen and letting them happen. At times grasping at an opportunity pushes it further away, while at other times, not grasping leads to missed opportunities.

Elisabeth Kubler-Ross, in her book *On Death and Dying*, identified a pattern of moods emerging from her numerous conversations with terminally ill people. She found that, when people first learned of their illness, their immediate reaction was to deny the inevitable. They would become angry and resentful as their attempts to lead a "normal" life became frustrated by their physical incapacity. Later, they would enter upon a period of bargaining, in the hope that they could somehow reverse things. Failure to do this would induce a mood of depression as they realized the futility of their struggles. For many, hitting rock bottom in this way, became a turning point—a point at which they accepted their impending fate and, from a mood of peace, set out to accomplish significant life goals in the limited time they had remaining.

In my own business, I have identified a similar pattern of moods emerging among quite healthy people working together in organized ways. The pattern of moods might be represented in the Figure 4–2.

If we look at the bottom left-hand box, we can see that battling against the odds results from denying the inevitability

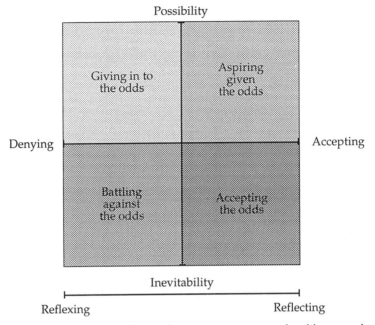

Figure 4–2   Patterns of moods emerging among healthy people working together in organized ways.

of a situation. It is usually our first reflexive "knee jerk" reaction when we can't get what we want. Typically, this invokes in us a mood of anger and frustration, as we fail at every turn. As time goes by, the mood of anger ultimately gives way to one of resignation as we accept the odds but feel powerless to do anything about it. Our struggling leaves us exhausted and clueless as to where to go next. We give up control of our lives to some force other than ourselves.

Further down the road, we become less reflexive and more reflective about our situation. We notice that help comes to us in unforeseen ways. Choice begins to play an increasing role in our decision to become hopeful about the possibility of being able to bring about some kind of change in our lives. We take on a mood of aspiration, seeking a new direction. Ultimately, with greater consciousness we are able to accept that, while there is much to be achieved in our lives, there are inevitable limitations to what can be accomplished. Some limitations we will be aware of; others will appear when we least expect them and, like the proverbial banana peel, will throw us to the ground.

When we both understand and remain open to both the inevitability and possibility in our lives, we give ourselves enormous capacity to grow and fulfill our limitlessness. We approach challenges with purpose and direction, and quiet our nagging internal voice telling us that nothing can be done. The key is to recognize and accept that, no matter how bad life seems, we always have choice.

MEMO

To: The Reader

From: Sean

Date: April 28th, 1996

Subject: Speaking from Experience

I can remember first reading Elisabeth Kubler-Ross's book and Martin Heidegger's treatise on mood in *Being and Time* and being shocked by the way their experiences matched my own.

When I was in my late teens, I lost my left foot following a serious climbing accident. Whilst recovering, I basically denied that my life would be any different. Once I was fitted with my prosthetic foot, I found the heavy wood and metal implement a poor substitute for my real foot. I could no longer run, so playing my favorite sport, rugby, was out of the question. Even long walks left me in agony. I eventually gave up the struggle, resigned to the fact that my life had become meaningless and there was nothing I could do about it. Alcohol became my companion and it wasn't long before my behavior became unacceptable to many people. I lost my friends, and my family was at a loss in knowing how to help me. The problem was that if I couldn't help myself, how could anyone else?

I eventually touched bottom and in coming to peace with the inevitability of my situation, my life began to turn around. I became determined to get back on track—a different track—and, out of nowhere, people began to show up in my life who helped me get to where I wanted to go.

I had no way of talking about my experience until I learned about mood.

Sean

As managers, coaches, teachers, parents, guardians, ministers, politicians, or presidents, it simply isn't enough to exhort people to accept your ideas and make the kinds of changes you want to make if their moods tend toward anger or resignation. Your challenge is to find ways to make it possible for people to name their moods, and to offer them alternatives. If you want to bring about a breakthrough in attitude of others, you must first alter the way those people perceive and understand the world—because their actions will always be perfectly correlated to these perceptions. Energy begets energy; thus, if you want people to share your aspirations, speak and act out of your aspiring mood.

The way people perceive the world is shaped by their internal and external conversations. Understanding people as *conversations* gives you access to altering the way the world occurs for them. They may be a conversation for being uncoordinated or for being graceful, for being untrainable or for being open to new thoughts. Once you consider them to be a conversation, you have access to performance. You can begin to change their view of the world by changing their conversation. Your presence has the potential to create a new context for your conversations. Oftentimes I have found that, people who have been written off as change-averse are merely short of a language to talk about their moods. By creating the space for them to express their anger or their resignation, they become more receptive to what you have to say and more able to spot the possibility in your aspirations. In my experience, most people aren't resistant to change but to being changed.

LOGIC AND LANGUAGE

In our day-to-day interactions with people, we engage in conversations without giving much thought to their effectiveness. Yet it is through our speaking and listening that we relate to one another. We make promises, we ask for things, we create an identity for ourselves, we manage teams, we fall in love, we run families, we direct projects. In short, we design and manage an intricate web of conversations which bring forth knowledge, generate commitment, and coordinate action.

Language is our distinctive way of being human. When we speak, we act in a special way; when we speak effectively, we have a profound impact on the world. The creative power of language lies in its capacity to bring forth distinctions from the undivided flow of life. Once, while driving home from a weekend's snowboarding in the mountains, my wife and children were engaged in a lively conversation about the dangers of driving at night with moose straying onto the road. There were signs posted at regular intervals telling us how many collisions had occurred so far that year. During a lull in the conversation, I decided to play a trick on them. I yelled "Moose!" and stepped on the brakes. At that very moment, everyone in the truck (with the exception of myself), saw a moose. My assertion had two sorts of meaning. On the one hand, it was a statement or report about events at a previous moment; on the

---

MEMO

To: The Reader

From: Sean

Date: April 20th, 1996

Subject: Language and Lemons

The story of the moose reminds me of a record my dad used to play when I was a kid. It was a recording of a man playing a trumpet on a street corner. A kid comes up to him and starts sucking on a lemon. The trumpet player tries desperately to continue playing, but eventually chases the kid off because he can't play anymore.

I have had the same effect on people when I describe the act of sucking a lemon. They begin to salivate. I have been able to make people wriggle in their seats by describing the sound of fingernails scraping down a blackboard.

It's amazing what you can do with words. In fact, every act of speaking is an act of manipulation. By speaking, you can move people's attention to where you want it to be. Speaking is action; committed speaking has the power to move people. The power to make a difference.

Sean

---

other hand, it was a command or stimulus for events at a later moment. I made a moose appear by simply saying so.

Our actions are perfectly coordinated with the way the world occurs to us. When we are creative we speak in ways that interrupt that coordination so that a new world comes into being. Introducing an interruption is an act of creating that brings things into existence (from the Latin *ex*, "out," and *sistere*, "to stand out") and makes the thinking of things possible. Attaining mastery in the art of speaking and listening is probably the most important challenge in our lives, because it is through our networks of conversations that we gain leverage on our actions. Through changing our conversations we invent new futures. This differs from our traditional clock logic approach that relies upon argument and critical reasoning as our primary instrument of change. Such an approach is virtually useless for change because it is founded on the mistaken belief that language, like other forms of expression, conveys information about *reality*. On the contrary, language offers much more because it is also a medium of expression that allows us to invent new ways of living and creating together.

If you carefully examine any action, you find there are always two sides to it: the side from which you can explain it, and the side from which you can produce it. For instance, in our earlier story of the snorkeler observing the submarine, it is quite possible for the snorkeler to describe accurately the movements of the submarine, but it is less likely the snorkler could climb inside and operate the vessel. While there is a relationship between the snorkeler's description of what the vessel is doing and what it is actually doing, the two are clearly not the same. As a describing system, language is excellent, but as a thinking system it is seriously flawed.

When we form power partnerships, we are serious about creating a future that isn't going to happen unless we do something. This doesn't mean that we should stop attempting to predict the future accurately; but power partnerships are designed to generate a future that was not predictable. For instance, the owner of a Harley-Davidson dealership once told me that, a few years ago, you could always tell a Harley in his showroom because it would be the one with a tray underneath the engine to catch the oil drips. How different the future might have been if someone at Harley-Davidson had tackled that problem then. As it happened, nobody foresaw the impending disaster that struck Harley-Davidson as once-loyal customers flocked to more competitively priced and higher-quality Japanese machines. The company had adopted a set of patterns that simply blinkered them from both the threats and the opportunities in their marketplace. Fortunately, they were able to recover and bounce back with a line of outstanding products that customers valued.

Language and Dichotomies

A second challenge of language is its natural capacity to create dichotomies. As I have mentioned throughout this book, our self-referencing nature places us in a tricky position when it comes to describing what we see "out there." Our descriptions can never be made independently from our perceptions because we are always *a part of* the world we describe, not *apart from* it. Consequently, when we attach meaning to phenomena, our descriptions are always in reference to ourselves. This means we automatically produce bipolar attributes which distinguish me from you, this from that, good from bad, us from them, subject from object, body from mind, good from evil, health from sickness. While such dichotomies are perfectly natural, they become mishandled when our attempts to ascribe meaning and significance to them result in our attributing value such that one of the terms dominates the other. In Jacques Derrida's words, "We are not dealing with the peaceful coexistence of a vis-à-vis, but rather with a violent hierarchy where one of the two terms dominates the other or has the upper hand." Consequently, me and you becomes me versus you, good and bad becomes good versus bad, us and them becomes us versus them, and so on.

This gives rise to crude and dangerous perceptions, and is the primary way we use language to contradict another's point of view. We have a tendency to think and talk as if the world were made up of separable parts. In our clock-logic world, scientists and philosophers have tried to discard from their language such words as "rather," "somewhat," "perhaps" and to avoid all forms of adjectives that end with "ish." They may not object to saying "this color is greyish," but they do not tolerate such expressions as "this proposition is "truish" or "rather true" or even "somewhat true." As Peter Senge and Fred Kofman (1995) point out:

> The analytic way to address a complex situation is to break it into components, study each component in isolation and then synthesize the components back into the whole. For a wide range of issues, there is little loss in assuming a mechanical structure and ignoring systemic iterations. But for the most important problems, linear thinking is ineffective. Problems like runaway costs in our health care system or the decline of a corporation's vitality and innovativeness resists piecemeal, analytic approaches. We live in a world more like Humpty Dumpty than a jigsaw puzzle: All the King's horses and all the King's men can't put the system together again.

As self-referencing systems, in order to know anything we must first distinguish ourselves from something else and we must also recognize that we also have the power to connect that which we separate. Douglas Flemmon (1991) puts it this way: "Not only from the first not a thing is but also from the first thing, a not is. Each side of a distinction—for example, assertion/denial, presence/absence, thing/no-thing—creates and is created by, the other." Each side exists by virtue of the difference that separates it from and connects it to its complement. Blindness to this simple realization characterizes not only our relationship to each other and our world, but also our relationship to ourselves. For instance, how many times have you heard someone say, "I can't stand people who don't value difference"? And how many times have you caught yourself in the act of blaming someone for blaming you? There is simply no way that logical argument can escape the "double bind" associated with language and communication from a self-referencing perspective.

We must explore this middle ground and create a whole new spectrum of perceptions. We must understand that a categorization under one set of circumstances does not hold under another. In power partnerships, we need a new language and way of thinking that cuts across dichotomies, changing "either/ors" into "both/ands." In Taoist philosophy this practice is known as W*u Wei* and is central to thinking from a both/and perspective. Benjamin Hoff (1982) translates the term as follows:

> Practically speaking, *Wu Wei* means without meddlesome, combative, or egotistical effort. It seems rather significant that the character *Wei* developed from the symbols for a clawing hand and a monkey, since the term *Wu Wei* means not going against the nature of things; no clever tampering; no "Monkeying Around."

I use the term "doing/not doing" to describe a way of experiencing and making sense of our worlds that is about acting in accord with context. As Mel Ziegler puts it, doing/not doing is "listening to what wants to happen by itself, not forcing it, not attempting to control, but only serving it by helping to remove the obstacles that are keeping it from happening." When designing our organizations as power partnering enterprises, we must design for the future we can predict and the future we must invent. This means creating systems and structures for doing/not doing that produce excellent products and services routinely, and that meets our commitments to a future we know. And we must design systems and structures that fit our commitment to a future we aspire to invent—a future that requires agility to respond to rapidly changing market conditions. We aspire to invent future of doing/not doing that bridges the dichotomy of stability versus agility, to give *stagility*.

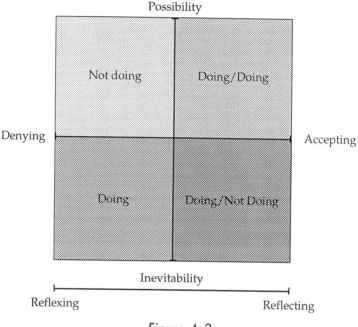

Figure 4–3

Using language in this way and practicing doing/not doing frees us from the chains of stereotypical meaning and enables us to invent entirely new possibilities for acting in the world. Being *stagile* means we can reframe our traditional perceptions of organizing, and create new images of organizations that can evolve, develop, and change in a fluid, self-organizing way. Power partnerships are stagile organizations, being sufficiently stable to provide excellent products and services routinely, while maintaining the agility to seize the rich patterns of opportunities as they emerge in the environment within which such partnerships operate.

LOGIC AND CONTEXT

On one of my frequent trips back home to England, I was struck by an advertisement for a vacuum cleaner made by a company called Electrolux. The caption read, "Nothing

Sucks Like an Electrolux." I couldn't help but wonder how successful this would be back in the United States. Similarly, I can remember, some years ago, seeing the equipment used on the first successful ascent of Everest by a British-led team of mountaineers. The equipment was on permanent display at an inn belonging to a friend. The inn was located in the heart of the Welsh mountains in the west of Britain, and had been used by the team while training for the Everest ascent.

On display was a very old and worn set of crampons, a pair of crusty boots, a rusty ice axe, a battered straw hat, and an old yellow oxygen tank. All pretty unimpressive stuff, really—except that, for me, they were the artifacts of the adventurer of my childhood dreams. As I gazed at the old equipment, memories flooded back of treks across glaciers, over high towering peaks, or exposed camps on the south col, in the teeth of howling winds and thundering avalanches. Such were the images I had created while nestling securely beneath warm blankets in the safety of my bedroom. These artifacts were personally meaningful because they been worn by my childhood hero, Sir Edmund Hillary, as he stood atop the highest mountain in the world. For the many people who have stayed at the hotel over the years, the display will have been viewed out of as many contexts. I know for a fact that, for the hotel staff who had to dust it each week, there reality was shaped by an entirely different context.

While visiting Kronberg Castle in Denmark, Niels Bohr is reputed to have said to fellow physicist, Werner Heisenberg:

> Isn't it strange how this castle changes as soon as one imagines that Hamlet lived here? As scientists, we believe that a castle consists only of stone and admire the way the architect put them together. The stones, the green roof, the patina, the wood carvings in the church constitute the whole castle. None of this should be changed by the fact that Hamlet lived there, and yet it is changed completely. Suddenly the walls and the ramparts speak a quite different language. The courtyard becomes an entire world, dark corners remind us of the darkness of the human soul, we hear Hamlet's "To be or

not to be." Yet all we really know about Hamlet is that his name appears in a thirteenth-century chronicle. No one can prove that he really lived, let alone that he lived here. But everyone knows the questions Shakespeare had him ask, the human depth he was made to reveal and so he too, had to be found a place on earth, here in Kronberg. And once we know that, Kronberg becomes quite a different castle for us.

Later, these men would show how even the most scientifically controlled experiments are shaped by the perceptions of the scientists involved.

The one essential element, common to all the factors that shape logic, is that they are contextual; that is, they derive their meaning from a background that is specific to the person making the meaning. As the late Carl Rogers (1980) pointed out:

> The only reality I can possibly know is the world as *I* perceive and experience it at this moment. The only reality you can possibly know is the world as *You* perceive and experience it at this moment. And the only certainty is that those perceived realities are different. There are as many "real worlds" as there are people! This creates a most burdensome dilemma, one never before experienced in history.

From time immemorial, the tribe, or the community, or the nation, or the culture has agreed upon what constitutes the real world. To be sure, different tribes and different cultures might have held sharply different world views, but at least there was a large, relatively unified group which felt assured in its knowledge of the world and the universe and knew that this perception was *true*.

Today we face a different challenge. The ease and rapidity of world-wide communication means that every one of us is aware of multiple *realities*, multiple contexts or backgrounds out of which people speak and act. I cannot stress too much the importance of valuing and sharing contexts because they shape the way the world occurs to us and consequently, the nature of our response to that world. Power partnerships recognize that certainty is not a proof of truth. They are based on the premise that the world we experience is not *the* world where perceptions and values are common, universal, permanent and agreed, but rather *a* world we bring forth with others. When we are in conflict with people who share our aspirations and who are critical to our success (as opposed to being with a group of dinner guests engaging in a lively discussion around a table), we must search for ways to value one another's perceptions, no matter how undesirable they may appear to us. Simply restating our position or making others wrong isn't going to change things. This is the essence of power partnering—bringing forth a world with others, through developing the capacity and capability to legitimize and value their perceptions so that, together, we can discover the limitless innovative possibilities out there waiting to be seized.

Knowing can never be taken out of context; to return to the examples mentioned above, the vacuum cleaner, the mountain equipment, and Kronberg Castle do not physically change. What makes them different is that we experience them through very different lenses, shaped by our mood, language, intention, and history; and it is this context that gives them meaning. Our challenge is to understand both our own context for knowing and those of the people with whom we wish to share our lives. For example, did you know that the context for designing your computer keyboard dates back to the early typewriter? The ridiculous positioning of the keys only makes sense when you understand that the context for typewriters was a keyboard designed to slow the typist down sufficiently enough to prevent adjacent hammers from jamming when accidentally struck simultaneously.

How much of your organization's culture is based on outdated contexts like the computer keyboard? How much is based upon patterns of meaning that once made sense but which, over time, have lost their meaning and relevance in today's business world? Like perishable goods, contexts have a "shelf life," a "sell by" date that requires continual turnover in order to remain fresh. Are your systems and structures designed to slow people down? Are your services and products meaningful in today's context—and will they remain so in the context of the new economy of the twenty-first century?

Becoming a power-partnering enterprise means finding ways to self-reflect continuously and to modify your perceptions and action repeatedly in light of new knowledge. It means becoming engaged in a continual effort to break the constraints of bureaucratic thinking and launch yourself into the reality of an Einsteinian world where capacities for continuous learning and self-organizing are the norm. While innovating through power partnering can be learned, it also must be allowed to arise directly, simply, and inevitably from our natural behavior as autonomous, pattern-generating, and recognizing systems. Many practical things can be developed from a good understanding and appreciation of context; power partnerships require a thorough understanding and appreciation of context in order to be of practical use.

Creating a New Logic 5

KNOWING HOW WE KNOW

I bought my son Nick a watch for his birthday. As he adjusted the hands, he said, "It's impossible to set the correct time because time is passing while I am moving the hands." While our perceptions and the systems of belief they form are our primary way of making sense of the world, they are also our way of concealing it. Reflecting is that precious moment when we pretend time stands still; for a split second, we dip our toes into a flowing stream of consciousness where past and future are lived in the present and an entirely new world appears before us.

As self-referencing systems the stream, by necessity, remains beyond our ordinary ability to comprehend. Yet it is nonetheless working for us in our inner world of perceptions and beliefs. Sometimes we can say that we know; other times, we just know that we know. Every reflection invariably takes place in language, which is our distinctive way of being human. We rarely attend to what we know, but rather to what we say we know about. We are aware of a certain kind of reality because it is the kind we can easily show and describe. We know far more than we can say, yet we have come to believe that what we can say is all we know.

In social settings we are guided by our beliefs and perceptions; we reflexively and reflectively monitor our own and other's actions based on them. Even though we know much more than we can say, all knowing is, in some way, designed to maintain a stable identity by ignoring or correcting deviations between what is and what should be. Our assertion of what should be is based on what we are up to at the time—and we are always up to *something*.

This way of thinking about thinking does not come naturally, yet understanding the unpredictable and ambiguous inner world of perception is critical if we are to become effective power partners. We are not always conscious of this process, yet it goes on all the time. We base our perceptions on patterns created through living in our world. Over time, these patterns become obvious, regular and acceptable. Since they do not require reflection to be generated, they are invisible unless they fail. Our main function in power partnerships is to cause this failure, because that is when reflection steps in.

While visiting Ireland recently, the reverse gear on my car broke; I was immediately transported to the world of reverselessness. In this world, none of my existing patterns of thinking and acting worked. I consistently parked my car as if I had a reverse gear and had to physically push it backward to go on my way. On another occasion, I went down a narrow road that ended at a beach. When I tried to go back the other way, I became hopelessly stuck across the road and had to seek the help of a nearby farmer to tow me out.

It takes special moments like this to short-circuit our normal patterns of perception and create entirely new insights. While many of us don't put it to good use, we each have evolved the capacity to reframe our reality in a way that allows us to modify our beliefs and perceptions to take account of new contexts. As we learn to value and take seriously one another's perceptions, we create a powerful synergy of insights. Power partnerships create an environment in which the sharing and valuing of each other's perceptions is encouraged, in order to engage our innate creativity. Through listening to and valuing the perceptions of others, we become dislodged from our traditional patterns of thinking and acting. If we are open to the possibility, a new world appears before our eyes—a world full of exciting new opportunities.

Power partnerships create the opportunity for insight because they are founded on a deep structure of valuing. Without this foundation, people divert their energy into second guessing the motives of other people, or simply dismissing them as having nothing special to add. This diversion kills the insights that lead to innovation because, as we have seen earlier, we can do remarkable things with words; and when we speak to ourselves and to others from a mood of devaluing, we remakably prevent anything new from occurring.

When we are insightful, we short-circuit existing thought patterns and literally create entirely new ones. The culture of valuing, that is the essence of power partnerships, enables the absorbing and sharing of perceptions that lead to insight. They bring us to new levels of consciousness that allow us to invent our futures, not merely react to them. Knowing how we know means we make things happen rather than watch them happen—or, worse still, be left scratching our heads wondering what happened. The challenge is to know how to value the beliefs and perspectives of other people. The challenge is to be a power partner in everything you do.

6

Power Partnering

CREATING CULTURES OF VALUING

Imagine you are head of the Royal Opera House in Covent Garden, London. A year ago, you granted unprecedented access to the BBC to film life as it really is behind the curtains of the nation's temple of high culture. A year ago, you felt uneasy when the program's producers said, "trust us." "If it is too controversial to screen, we agree to leave it out," they assured you. When the first episode aired on television, your worst fears were realized as the British public was treated to the spectacle of chaotic managers, brutal firings, and collapsing divas. The most venomous performance was by your director of public affairs who, having thrown the telephone to the floor in a fit of pique, yelled the immortal line, "Sod it, the House will actually do what I determine it will do."

In the latest episode, you are in the limelight as you receive verbal maulings from a taxi driver and members of your board. At the center of the storm is a decision which your ballet chairman condemns as "appalling incompetence." Only one person has been contracted to design sets and costumes for a new opera and ballet opening within days of each other. Both sets are late. Overexpenditures loom. "Absolutely catastrophic.

Words fail me," chokes your board chairman. To add to the storm, the megastar director of your company's newest production demands a complete re-design of the set. He wants rain, collapsing scenery and live shire horses, which promptly cobble the stage with excrement. "These grand people!" rants your opera chairman. "They really are bastards." Indignantly your director says he is "sickened at being called a bastard" and deplores the chairman's comments. With four more episodes to go you cringe at the thought of what will come next and wonder at the wisdom of your decision to do the program in the first place.

This is a true story. Does it sound familiar? Has it ever happened to you? In my business I see this pattern repeated time and time again—in a variety of businesses, in a variety of countries around the world. What amazes me even more is that, in many cases, these dysfunctional patterns are so inculturated they take on a kind of life of their own. The worst thing one can do with such organizations is attempt to enter into a power partnership with them; such a relationship would only cause people in this sort of organization to become confused and angry. Paradoxically, the shadow side of autonomy, freedom, discretion, and authorization is, for some people, a sense of loss of control and greatly increased uncertainty.

While many people talk about the advantages and importance of valuing in the workplace, they typically attach a "but" to their assertions. "Oh yes, we really see the importance of valuing—but it could never happen here." Sadly, when the world appears this way to us, we leave ourselves no access to a new world unfolding for us. It is a crying shame that we settle for mediocracy when it comes to tapping into the vast reserves of knowledge lying dormant in our companies—when companies as prestigious as the Royal Opera House, simply brimming with talent, keep that talent trapped within a culture of devaluing. Is it possible that the force of such a culture can prevent a talent-laden organization from ever being transformed into vibrant and creative action?

When we reinvent ourselves as power-partnering enterprises we make it possible for conversations to take place that produce insight and innovation as a matter of routine. We design our conversations in ways that bring people together in the spirit of partnership. We infuse people with a common sense of purpose and, from that connectedness, people enjoy the freedom to invent new possibilities and bring them into being. If you think this sounds good, but don't believe it can ever happen in "real life," consider the following example.

The "Republic of Tea" is a purveyor of award-winning teas and earned its first dollar in 1992. Since then the company has seen its revenues increase exponentially. Nowhere is the passion for power partnering been more clearly expressed than in the book *The Republic of Tea*, in which Mel and Patricia Ziegler, co-creators of Banana Republic, and Bill Rosenzweig, CEO of the Republic of Tea, present a vivid portrait of the creative process required to launch yet another tea company. The book opens with Mel Ziegler describing his first encounter with Bill Rozenzweig as the two men head for home from a conference:

> After checking out of my hotel, I found myself sharing a car to the airport with a young man who had been attending the conference and was leaving early to make a meeting in San Francisco. As it turned out, we were on the same flight. We struck up a conversation that became so quickly intense that it obliterated everything else around us as we negotiated through the check-in and boarded the aircraft. We immediately rearranged our seats so we could sit together. Strangers on a plane speeding at 35,000 feet across America, we found ourselves in the grip of an energy that was clearly overtaking us. Whatever the energy was, it had us spinning in the vortex of a creative zone. We were in a highly charged no-man's-land, outside space and time, where The Source of an Idea was revealing itself to us in its yet unborn state. Time and space reappeared seven hours later when we looked up and saw that the plane, on the ground, in San Francisco was empty. By then it was apparent that The Idea had been born—in us.

The key point Ziegler (1992) makes is that the idea didn't come from nowhere; rather, it existed in the inner worlds of both men as an internal pattern waiting to be triggered. "The Idea existed but had not *manifested*. It was as a projection looking for a screen," Ziegler wrote. He continued:

> The great mystery we know as the "creative process" is, in fact, the stirring of the unborn in its search for a friendly place to be born. It is awesome enough to find oneself engaged alone with the process. But it is truly imposing when the process visits two or more people simultaneously.

So how can we transform our organizations into friendly places in which the unborn creative ideas might find a place to be born? What have we learned so far that provide us with an indication of the necessary ingredients for outstanding power partnerships?

7

Characteristics of Successful Power Partnerships

Having reached this point in the book, it is now time to review what has been said and to distill from its essence the criteria that are vital to initiating and sustaining successful power partnerships. What have we learned about the nature of reality that points to some clues about the characteristics of power partners? What have we learned about the nature of reality that points to some clues about the characteristics of power partners? What qualities do they bring to their relationship that generate the kind of relentless perseverance that transforms an innovative idea into something really special and unique?

We began by looking at the way advanced electronic communication systems are making possible the formation of an entirely new economy based on the networking of human knowledge. Along the way, we proposed that this new knowledge era would challenge us to look for ways to leverage the knowledge of all those people involved in the success of our companies. Whether they be co-workers, suppliers, customers, our customer's customers, or our local and national community, each—in their own way and collectively—possess the knowledge that allows us to invent futures that would not otherwise happen without their committed and knowledgeable participation with us.

It was our considered opinion that, for many companies, being proactive was no longer a matter of choice, but an essential part of being a successful player in the new knowledge economy of the twenty-first century. We asserted that the increasing pace of change could no longer be understood using prevailing mechanistic, authoritarian, clock logic models based on separateness and privileged access to information. What we needed, we said, was nothing short of an entirely new logic, based on values of interrelatedness and free access to information where ambiguity, confusion, and anxiety were the primary initiators of new learning, awareness, and action.

This key to the success of this new reverse logic, we said, was its ability to shift our normal patterns of perception in ways that created entirely new insights. We believed that, by dynamically networking these insights together with people we value, we would dislodge ourselves from our routine patterns of thinking and acting and create a powerful synergy of insights that would broaden our horizons and reveal entirely new worlds full of exciting possibilities.

So what have we said so far that might provide us with a blueprint for initiating and sustaining successful power partnerships? I will go over our findings briefly here and then, in the second part of the book, cover them in greater detail. Themes emerging from our discourse so far indicate that successful power partnerships display the following characteristics:

1. Power Partnerships consist of people who have shared aspirations concerning the future they intend to invent. This means that, from the very beginning, they engage in conversations designed to surface old issues and grievances, and to gain closure on them. They do not accept that such situations should be left unresolved because they know that, until they are, their partnership will be constantly haunted by these ghosts. Power partners have no uncertainty about the vision they are working towards. The future they have declared for themselves is the future they all passionately wish to bring about.

2. In power partnerships, people represent a level of diversity that leads to difference with deference. Without deferring their strongly held beliefs, power partners know that they will miss the subtle cues that bring forth insight. Without diversity, they know they run the risk of creating harmony rather than discord. Without discord, they know there is no energy to challenge existing assumptions and create entirely new ones. Different skills, different access to specific information, different elements of knowledge, different genders, races, colors creeds, ages, and histories, all contribute to the creative process—so long as they exist in a culture of valuing. Power partners know it is essential to create valuing discourse if they are to innovate and bring their creative ideas into the world. They engage in conversations specifically designed to create cultures of valuing and shared commitment. Their conversations are ongoing because they know that they can only speak about a small percentage of what they value and are committed to. They know that their true values will appear as they struggle to fulfill their commitments and consequently, must never be taken for granted.

3. Power partnerships exist in environments of available information. Power Partners are free to come together wherever and whenever necessary. This doesn't always mean face-to-face interaction. Conversations can take place using the myriad of electronic communicating technologies currently available. This leads us to another important, related characteristic: power partnerships have free access to the best technology there is. For instance, meeting rooms are designed to enable creativity. They are equipped with "eye muscle" tools, such as wall-to-wall white boards, flip-chart pads, cameras that photograph whole walls of drawings, and so forth. Power partners engage in conversations specifically designed to discover possibilities. Theirs are unconstrained conversations

in which all ideas are considered relevant, all suggestions taken seriously. It is only when all avenues have been explored that criteria are introduced to scope out those possibilities the partners wish to act upon.

4. Power Partnerships are not just about talk; they are also about action. Conversations, once they have been through the stages mentioned above, are about transforming innovative ideas into leading-edge products and services. Power partners engage in conversations specifically designed to create action. These conversation have speakers and hearers, but both are listening. Clearly stated and agreed-upon goals and objectives combine with equally clearly stated conditions of satisfaction such as time and cost guidelines. There is a shared belief that the goals can be achieved, clearly stated requests and sincere promises.

In the second part of this book we will explore each of these characteristics in greater detail.

Part 2

Power Partnering Teknowledgies

The first part of the book was concerned with the nature, logic, and importance of power partnering. This second part is concerned with the *teknowledgies* that transform the principles of power partnering into a powerful strategy for organizational success. In the third part of the book, I will focus on the practical application of power partnering teknowledgies within organizations.

Power-partnering teknowledgies are concerned with generating insightful and innovative ideas and transforming them into leading-edge products and services that delight your customers and continually differentiate you from your competition. The process works because it defines the context for power partnering, enabling people to operate within a common framework of meaning. Like the rules of a game, each player knows how the game is played and the various phases through which the game progresses. The power partnering framework provides a shared and agreed-upon set of lenses through which to view your world, making it easier for you to recognize situations and act appropriately and effectively. Just like a production worker at Ford stopping the line when a defect is spotted, the power partnering framework makes it possible for you to interrupt the smooth flow of action to complain for new action or an alternative mode of thinking. It's the point at which you say, "There's an opportunity emerging that needs further exploration. Let's create a power partnership with our customers and listen with intention and attention to what they have to say." This is what the people at Steelcase did when they collaborated with their customers to uncover innovative ideas that enhanced their productivity and effectiveness. Their insights led to the creation of their "Personal Harbor" workspaces, an environment designed to encourage interaction among people.

Similarly, when we are in hot pursuit of a great idea and our organizational structures get in the way of progress, we can ask for some green-lens partnering to create new ones. Promoting new ways of thinking that lead to surprising perspectives and innovative ideas cannot be performed outside of your overarching organizational context. Yellow lenses provide us with a perspective through which to agree on our purpose and values. They set up the context for action. Furthermore, action must be strategic and guided by plans that are meaningful in time yet flexible through time as contexts change. As with everything in power partnering, you can never assume that today's plans will be relevant tomorrow. At times we must wear our black lenses to shield our eyes from the brightness of too much innovating. We must be sufficiently stagile to take on innovative ideas while maintaining overall direction. Like a compass bearing, stagile planning keeps our sailboat heading west even though the wind is hitting us head on—causing us to tack in different directions in order to move ahead.

There will be times when too much aspiring impacts your ability to produce high-quality products and services routinely. When this becomes an issue, the framework makes it possible for you to complain for appreciation—asking that people don't loose sight of commitments already made. It is at such times when we must pause to say, "We appear to have forgotten our core purpose and strategic goals. I feel we should take some time to appreciate why we embarked on this journey in the first place. Our people are spread too thin; unless we do something, it won't be long before we start breaking our commitments to our customers."

The phases in the framework don't necessarily need to take place sequentially. The sequence will vary depending on the situation. For instance, listening appreciatively to someone's account of their vision will often cause you to reconsider your own. Moreover, when you trust someone enough to share your vision and goals, you increase the likelihood that they will reciprocate, thereby increasing the level of trust existing between you. Energy begets energy; valuing one another in this way increases the free flow of information which, in turn, increases the exchange of knowledge. Information acquired in this way is the critical ingredient in power partnering because it makes possible the mutual creation of new insights and innovative possibilities for all involved. The framework is made up of four lenses:

ASPIRING

The clear partnering lenses represent clear thinking. Aspiring is about clearing your mind of old biases and assumptions and intentionally listening for possibilities. Aspiring is concerned with creating a mood of purpose that acts like a radio antenna, drawing innovative ideas out of the ether and encoding their signals into a language you can understand. Your challenge is to create a power-partnering culture where people routinely leverage one another's unique creative talents to solve problems and invent leading edge products and services. They work in an environment where people genuinely value and trust one another. The process begins with an assessment of the competitive environment within which your enterprise intends to operate. With the help your suppliers, your customers, and your customer's customers in dynamic, innovative, and co-creative relationships, you will discover the possibilities existing in your marketplace—which, if seized, offer outstanding opportunity.

IMAGINING

The yellow partnering lenses represent bright sunlight. Imagining provides the illumination required to see your innovative idea in action. Your insights provide the foundation upon which you craft your mission and operating philosophy. This is the context that will guide your future thinking and acting. It will be used to establish a sense-in-common, among all those who are invested in the success of your enterprise. Declaring and maintaining your context provides a cause-in-common around which members of your enterprise can gather and sustain the kind of belief without evidence required in the early stages of any bold venture. If aspiring is about opening your mind to new possibilities, imagining sheds light on the future you are about to make happen. Imagining illuminates the strategic plans that will transform your innovative ideas into winning products and services. Imagining engages you in sketching them out, visualizing them, and understanding the changes required to make them happen.

Imagining maps your innovative ideas into the minds and hearts of people who do not share your perceptions and beliefs, in order to gain their trust and support in the feasibility, value, and acceptance of your ideas. After all, any creative idea worth its salt will initially attract critics who will tell you it's a bad idea—because it doesn't match the world as they know it. Understanding their worlds is critical to the successful implementation of your idea. This phase is concerned with concentrating the minds of others on the task at hand through setting your own example.

CREATING

The green partnering lenses represent growth—the budding of your innovative ideas into trees that will bare fruit. Guided by the overarching context of your business and your strategic plans, an organizational architecture is crafted that is aligned with this context, bringing social, operational, informational and technical processes, systems, and structures into alignment. Your challenge is to build an organization that is stagile—giving you the stability to produce excellent products and services routinely, while at the same time being agile enough to take advantage continually of ever-emerging business opportunities.

Stagility enables communities of knowledge workers to operate in an environment of interconnectivity, supported by information tools and technologies, such as decision-support software, multimedia presentations and active computer networking. This environment enhances knowledge sharing and innovating. These systems are not means unto themselves, but are in place to serve people who have a compelling reason to share their knowledge.

TRANSFORMING

Black partnering lenses vary the degree of illumination required to nurture your idea. Black also represents dying in order to be reborn. Black partnering lenses ensure that thinking and acting remains aligned with your organizational context. Anything that does not support this context must be weeded out. Transforming ensures that every step in the process is supported by systems and structures that are enabling, and that all the people invested in the success of your business are capable of achieving that success. Transforming is about dying in order to be reborn—which requires constant vigilance against complacency. Capability is developed through a strategic learning system that focuses on building talent through teaming and re-teaming competencies. These clusters of competencies are held together by a deep structure of trust and openness where people willingly share information and build on each other's aspirations and abilities. In this way, learning and sharing knowledge becomes a permanent and natural aspect of running your business.

Strategic learning develops a spirit of innovation. It helps people learn ways to become efficient and flexible, to plan strategically and adapt swiftly to the unexpected—exactly the same skills required to run your business. In fact, strategic learning mirrors those practices so that learning and working are inextricably linked. Strategic learning goals, reflecting the goals of your business, are typically characterized by their clarity of vision and the focus of their mission on the customer and a commitment to continuous improvement.

Transforming shifts your culture from one that solves problems to one that continually seeks opportunities. You create an environmental mindset that values the strengths and capabilities of others, builds upon them, and becomes enlightened and enriched by the process. Transforming maintains appreciation for the task at hand and unites those people who are committed to its success.

THE POWER PARTNERING FRAMEWORK

When combined, the lenses form a framework for power partnering in any situation. This framework is not a static process where completing the cycle brings you instant success. It is, as John Dewey (1929) pointed out, "a continual and intentional process of discovering insights, producing action, observing the consequences, and adapting behavior." It is a process of *becoming* in time and through time, in which each journey brings new insights, knowledge, and capability, while moving you progressively closer to fulfilling your potential. The challenge is to establish for yourself a culture that focuses on discovering the talents and capabilities of people through genuinely valuing one another and building relationships of trust.

Now, let's take a closer look through each power-partnering lens.

8

Aspiring:
Engaging Your Creative Potential

When faced with complexity, we make life easy by making things routine. After all, it makes good sense to use our brain's natural capacity to form routine patterns of thinking and behaving. Unfortunately, routines maintain the status quo. When we are in the business of out-innovating our competition, aspiring is an effective way of interrupting our routine patterns, causing new conversations to take place about exciting new possibilities. Once identified, these possibilities illuminate the gap between where we are and where we want to be. Aspiring defines what is missing, and the strategy and operating philosophy for success. It establishes a context for your work, a common sense of purpose and valuing among those invested in that success. It provides the focus, force, and direction required for our enterprise to fulfill its potential. Five key elements are viewed through the Aspiring Lens:

LISTENING

The fictional detective Sherlock Holmes attributed his exceptional powers of detection to observing. As he told his faithful companion Dr. Watson, "ordinary people see, but I observe." Listening is concerned with exploring, investigating, and collecting clues. The process of listening is about gathering information and discerning patterns of opportunity before anyone else. In most organizations today, listening has taken a back seat to the more predominant practice of telling. Power partnering is an attempt to reverse this trend by turning down the volume on your inner dialogue, speaking only to gain clarity and listening to people in ways that bring meaning to seemingly complex streams of ideas.

This doesn't mean you listen without purpose, but rather that you don't let your purpose drown out what others are saying. Listening in this way means skillfully allowing new pieces of information to trigger thinking about their relationship with information you already know. This would be analogous to searching for an answer to a clue in a crossword puzzle. Once found, the answer reappears in the most unlikely places. It was always there; you just weren't looking for it.

MEMO

To: The Reader

From: Sean

Date: April 21st, 1996

Subject: Treading on a Crossword Solution

I had been searching my mind for the answer to this crossword clue: "Early device in British prisons for exercise." The answer was on the tip of my tongue, and yet I couldn't get it. What frustrated me even more was the fact that I had lived in an old garrison town in Wales that had a Victorian prison in the center of town. The place was now a museum, which I had visited; I could remember seeing the "early device for exercise," yet still couldn't put a name to it. *I wanted that clue so badly.*

Then, last night, at dinner with friends, the conversation got onto exercise routines. Someone said, "I have an exercise routine that works for me and fits my busy life-style. I have a treadmill in my bedroom and I do a forty-minute workout each morning."
There was the answer. I had solved the puzzle by intentionally *setting my mind to it* and placing the question in the back of my mind. Sure enough, the answer came to me; I didn't have to consciously go looking for it.

Sean

In the same way, you may be searching for a unique product or service that differentiates you from your competitors. This is your purpose, this is what you intend; while you know a great deal about what you don't want, you find it impossible to put your finger on what it is you *do* want. Through listening, you intentionally place your question in the back of your mind with a flag on it saying, "information needed." In so doing, you make it possible for the information to come to you from some of the most unlikely places. For example, you might be strolling through a library, or meeting someone—and your brain will suddenly flag the fact that the information you have been waiting for has arrived.

You knew it all along and, rather than push for a solution, you simply removed the barriers preventing your creative idea from emerging. Listening is essential to innovative thinking because it interrupts your routine patterns of practice. Your mind only sees what it is prepared to see and notices what it is ready to notice. Like pathways crisscrossing a playing field, once formed, experience follows these patterns just as people follow the pathways to cross the field. Your brain does an excellent job at using these patterns to react quickly to challenges and crisis. Listening creates the space for you to operate without meddlesome, combative, or egotistical effort. With your mind prepared in this way, you go with the nature of things and enter a world where opportunities appear coincidentally.

In power partnerships, you listen to others from your shared commitment to a particular purpose. Whenever you are up to something big in your life, you ask questions like:

"Where have I been?"

"Where am I going?"

"What's missing?"

"How will I go about finding it?"

"How will I know when I have found it?"

There are things you know you know, things you know you *don't* know, and things you *don't* know you don't know. When you enter into power partnerships with people whom you value and who share your aspirations, you are in special company; you are with people who are asking similar questions, and who have varying degrees of knowledge about certain things just like you do.

Listening to one another intently, from your mutual commitment to a bigger purpose, leads to insight through valuing your differing perceptions and beliefs and deferring your own deeply held beliefs. In this way you discover entirely new and creative ideas and combine your talents to transform them into innovative products and services. In the case of your customers, when you know and appreciate where they are going and how they intend to get there, you place yourself in the best possible position to anticipate their future needs and create innovative ways to help fulfill them.

For example, a firm in Boston created an advertising campaign for Volkswagen that led to 20 percent increase in sales over the previous year. Also, awareness of Volkswagen's products jumped more in six months than in the previous five or more years. This happened because the design team set out to create an advertisement that Volkswagen's customers and prospective customers would immediately identify with. Through listening to their customer's customer, the team compiled a profile of a VW owner. The profile described a person who:

- Is under 35
- Goes on exciting road trips even if they are married
- Has the sun roof open even if it does mess up their hair
- Likes reliability and practicality but also wants to have fun
- Likes to play loud music in their car.

From this profile, the team created a series of advertisements entitled "Drivers Wanted," that captured the imagination of thousands of people. A good many of these were people who may never have imagined themselves behind the wheel of a VW, until the advertisement placed them there. The advertising team successfully leveraged the knowledge and aspirations of their customer's customer to create an innovative advertising campaign which, by definition, nobody had thought of before.

Power partnerships thrive where there is a solid foundation of mutual understanding and valuing of each other's aspirations, challenges and abilities. Once in place, this foundation makes it possible to strengthen and enhance these relationships to produce innovative products and services that achieve sustained competitive and collaborative advantage. Power partnerships are shaped by the interplay of potential, ability, and the influence of time, caused by the nature of the market environment within which they exist. For example, if your company operates in a highly stable market environment where very little changes over time, then you will probably gain little from power partnering. This is often the case in companies that generate revenue by giving their customers what they want. In these cases, their customer has figured out what they want and do not want to be presented with, or be helped to discover for themselves, other options. This leads to stable self-referencing relationships where nothing innovative ever happens, nor ever needs to happen.

On the other hand, in situations where your company has big aspirations but finds itself severely constrained by complexity and time pressures, power partnering is essential because it turbo-charges your performance by increasing your ability to innovate. When you become masterful at innovating you literally expand time by making the best use of space. Take, for example, the challenges of learning to play tennis. For a beginner, the opposite court looks like the size of a postage stamp, the net as high as a billboard and the ball a pea traveling at twice the speed of sound. As you become more skilled, the net shrinks in size, the opposite court expands to the size of a football field, and the ball floats over the net leaving you plenty of time to deliver the perfect shot.

When you make power partnering a way of life, you will continually amaze yourself by your achievements. As with tennis, once you have mastered this game, you will wonder what else is possible. You will constantly expand your horizons, rather than fearing you will fall over the edge of them. Understanding these key elements provides a topographical map of the territory and a continual assessment of the potential and capabilities of your enterprise to reach its ever-changing destination. Likewise, understanding these same elements as they relate to your customers and their customers will enhance your capacity to become an integral part of their success.

PURPOSING

Purposing causes you to pause for a while to consider what you are actually doing and compare it with what you want to be doing. Purposing makes explicit what must be put in place, and what roadblock must be removed, in order for you to reach your aspirations. Purposing paves the way for later planning conversations where strategic objectives and goals are determined. Purposing establishes the context for your thinking and a feel for your action. Sharing your context with others allows them to talk about their hidden assumptions and reshape them to support the task at hand.

Purposing allows the hundreds of possibilities raised by your listening process to be shaped by your organizational context. You select only those that fit within this context and that you are willing and committed to pursue. Purposing provides the compass bearing that guides the long-term direction of your enterprise, no matter what terrain you encounter along the way or what winds blow you off course. Purposing engages the will and spirit of people through creating sufficient tension between aspirations and abilities to capture their imagination.

Purposing is not envisioning. While both are intended to produce creative tension between existing circumstances and ultimate possibilities, the latter brings shape to innovative possibilities while the former maintains the overarching context of your enterprise, enduring in time, through time and outside of time. Purposing is powerful because it maintains the fundamental reason-for-being of your enterprise and engages the will and spirit of people as they continually adapt to the new opportunities emerging from the listening process. A compelling purpose keeps the dream alive when the banana peels appear underfoot.

Purposing transforms possibilities into realities while, at the same time, engaging the will and commitment of people. This is analogous to planting a seed in the ground. Once beneath the surface, the seed is invisible to all but those who planted it. Only the gardener knows and believes in the seed's potential to transform into a beautiful flower. Until something visible appears, the gardener must provide a compelling articulation of the seed's potential. For instance, when creating his Sundance company, the famous film star Robert Redford described the process in the following way: "Sometimes things happen by design, sometimes by accident, many times by luck. When all three of these factors are joined by relentless perseverance, you have Sundance." With a clear mission of nurturing new art and bringing it to a wider audience, and no clear idea of how to do it, Redford recalls:

> I set out to create a special place. The goal was a working retreat for artists developed in harmony with the environment. A place where the public would be welcome so that the experience would be available to all those who cared to seek it out. Many interesting things happened along the way— some great successes and many failures. But that process of discovery through trial and error, the freedom to try something new and fail is a part of what Sundance is about today.

While there are many ways to go about purposing, the key elements that nurture your innovative project are:

- Valuing
- Information-sharing and knowledge-networking
- An appreciation for the context of your work and a willingness to align your actions to it.

If you reflect on the criteria for successful power partnerships, outlined in the first part of this book, you will see how multiple perceptions and beliefs are essential to the innovating process just so long as there is a strong commitment to valuing one another, the context of your work, and the potential, purposes, and capabilities of people. For instance, one of my clients asked me to help him solve a problem concerning his company's use of chlorofluorocarbons (CFCs). He was highly sensitive to the impact his company had on the environment; he had learned about the connection between CFC emissions and global warming, and wanted to know the extent to which his company was contributing to this problem. He initiated a study the conclusions of which found that, while they were using CFCs in their manufacturing process, their consumption was well within the guidelines laid down by the Montreal Protocol. This didn't satisfy him and he put a program in place to eliminate all CFC usage within twelve months. A project team was formed using power-partnering guidelines, and its members immediately set about understanding the extent of the challenge.

They convened a conference to set the context for the work. They invited key customers, suppliers, community representatives, and people from within the company who shared their concerns and believed they had something to offer that would lead to the discovery of an alternative to CFCs. Because of the level of commitment people felt towards overcoming the challenge, it wasn't necessary to manage the project in the traditional sense of the word. A leadership team of senior managers was put in place in order to remove any roadblocks, coordinate the work of the various project teams, and make sure they had the necessary processes and systems in place to enable information to flow and knowledge to be exchanged. As one manager put it:

> If you have a collaborative kind of effort, you have to have people who keep announcing what your mission is. Like those "fly-by-wire" aircraft, where you have to have somebody

steering the thing all the time or it will fall out of the sky. There seems to be a lot of things in this life that you just have to keep feeding energy into just to keep it on a level plane.

Self-managing teams formed and re-formed as progress got underway. For example, while a university student, one young engineer had attended a few courses on "droplet technology" before joining the company. She felt confident that the module cleaning process, which had previously used CFCs, could be successfully replaced by a solution of soap and water delivered under high pressure. The challenge was to deliver the solution with sufficient force to remove solder residue, but not so strong as to blow the delicate electronic components off the board.

A team was formed to investigate the matter and, to their surprise, they found that the best place to go for help was a company that manufactured fire sprinkler heads. Unfortunately, while this company could design and produce nozzles for the cleaning process, they didn't have the ability to deliver the water solution under high pressure. Using the groupware program Lotus Notes, the team shared their concerns. One of the conference members, sitting in an office on the other side of the country, joined in the conference by way of Lotus Notes and told the other team members that he had once worked for a company in Wisconsin, when he was a student, that produced equipment for cleaning dairy appliances by delivering a heated suspension of soap and water under pressure.

The leadership team brought together technologists from both companies and borrowed space in a manufacturing facility to set up a prototype machine. Innovation followed innovation and eventually the team delivered a prototype machine on time and below budget that could clean computer modules as effectively as the CFC process but without endangering the environment. The company patented the design and then gave it away to another company that had the will and capability to build machines on a larger scale.

VALUING

The health care industry is undergoing radical restructuring today—brought on largely by insurance companies who, in an attempt to reduce dramatically the cost of patient care, are mandating shorter hospital stays and making other crucial decisions about patient care. Somewhere along the way, the context for delivering health care changed. The emphasis shifted from quality of care at any cost to quality of care at the lowest cost. The result has been a gradual deterioration in the quality and range of choices offered to customers. More than ever, the customer today must indeed be patient.

In an attempt to focus attention on the original context for health care delivery, Dr. Arnold Relman, former editor of the *New England Journal of Medicine*, observed (*Boston Business Journal*, 1996): "We are in the unique and distinct business of helping the vulnerable. No business nor industry has greater obligations and those of us who work in health care must hear the powerful message and remember the simple truth: that our industry exists to care."

When you commit yourself to power partnering, you commit yourself and your company to a context no less vital than that espoused by Dr. Relman. You are committing yourself to a course of action and a set of beliefs that value people and these values form the context of your business. The essence of power partnering is valuing. Whenever I ask people what makes for a successful relationship in business they tell me many things, but the one quality that consistently ranks first is the importance of valuing one another. For instance, one person told me:

> I believe passionately in the power of working together. I expect complete cooperation from my suppliers because I believe they are working for our success. The better we do, the better they do and the more we value them, the more successful will be the relationship. I believe most people want

to be honest and sharing and maybe because I believe that, that is what comes my way.

When I asked members of the CFC elimination program why they felt the program met (and in many cases, exceeded) expectations, they were unanimous. In their opinion, the program worked because people were highly committed to achieving the end result—and because they valued one another throughout the program. "Valuing ourselves, valuing others, and others valuing us," they said.

Without this essential element, there can be no power partnering. With it, relationships with your partners, customers, and suppliers will thrive and grow from the loyalty you create through establishing relationships that are mutually valuing. The open communication this fosters is the fuel for innovation and creativity. It is healthy, it's fun, and it downright feels good. When you gather all the energy it takes to mistrust and devalue others and turn it into positive creative energy, you become unstoppable.

Without valuing, the creative energy of your organization becomes sucked into a vortex of devaluing and distrust that leaves little room for innovating. Nowhere is this more evident than in organizations dealing with the aftermath of downsizing, reengineering, or both. People who survived the layoffs now face increased workloads and reduced paychecks. Many feel guilty that they survived while their colleagues did not. They feel trapped and powerless to bring about any positive change; for many, the threat of further downsizing looms over their heads. In such environments there can be little room for trusting and even less room for valuing. Creativity is something to be saved for the weekend; the task at hand is to survive. Is it any wonder that our new lean and mean organizations are not experiencing the results promised by their reengineers?

So why is valuing such a big deal? After all, are we not a nation of rugged individualists? Didn't our frontier heritage account for anything? According to Erik Erikson, our need to value others and to be valued has its roots in our psychosocial development, especially the anxiety-provoking stimulus of the mother's periodic separation and return. Erikson says (*Childhood and Society*, 1963): "The infant's first social achievement is his willingness to let the mother out of sight without undue anxiety or rage, because she has become an inner certainty as well as an outer predictability. Such consistency, continuity, and sameness of experience provides a rudimentary sense of ego identity."

From a psychosocial perspective, valuing is an artifact from our unconscious need for security, formed early in life and is inextricably linked to our need for predictability and recognition throughout our lives. While valuing occurs naturally in some cases, it is more often achieved through attaining a level of consistency between what you say and what you do. Depending upon how sensitive you are or how sensitive the situation is, you have a kind of built-in sixth sense that can sniff out the intentions of others. As one manager told me:

> You have to value unconditionally, to put your negative assessments up on the shelf and value the other person. That doesn't mean you wont get stepped on every now and again, but when you do you brush yourself off and you get right back in there with them again—and eventually they will value you. The alternative is, they find out that you don't value them therefore they don't value you. This means they become cautious and you respond with more caution. Eventually the only thing we do is become increasingly cautious with one another and nothing gets done.

This doesn't mean throwing all caution to the wind and blindly leaving yourself wide open to people with evil intent. It does, however, mean avoiding the heavy doses of devaluing and distrust that have become so much a part of our contemporary way of life. It means holding open the window of possibility between accepting and eliminating someone a little longer than usual in order to hear, understand, and value the other person's point of view. Without deference, you leave little room for improvement because you play your relationships safe. Power partnering deliberately challenges existing assumptions to uncover new patterns of meaning and possibility. You need a solid foundation of valuing before this can happen.

When you value someone, you trust them. You trust in their ability to enrich your life in some way, and you value them for this. Likewise, when you trust someone, you value their ability to fulfill a request you have made that will, in some way, enrich your life. All valuing is trusting, and all trusting is valuing. The two are inextricably linked. The value of a trusting relationship lies in your ability to make requests of people and to rely on the strength of their promise to deliver something at a future time. This is the foundation of any successful relationship, and the essence of power partnering.

9

Imagining:
Shaping the Future Together

Imagining is concerned with providing a friendly place for new ideas to be born. It is about making them manifest in a way that captures the imagination of those who will be responsible for helping you bring your ideas to life. The products and services you create will be a work of art accomplished by people who share your aspirations and value your approach to being in the world. What you produce will be an expression of that relationship, a manifestation of their collective wisdom—and therefore, greater than any one individual. As we asserted in the first part of the book, we exist only in relationship to one another. Consequently, the whole power partnering process, from listening and purposing to valuing and envisioning, is an ongoing exploration of your interconnectedness to each other, to your customers, to your suppliers, to your co-workers—to everyone you deal with as you bring your innovative ideas to life. Imagining forms your identity with these people and shapes the context for all future action.

Imagining is the most critical stage because identifying and proposing anything new carries with it an inherent risk of failure. It is inevitable that people will have difficulty seeing the problem and solution, or conceptualizing the new idea, in the same way you do. Their mental picture of your problem and their mental picture of your solution almost always mismatch, simply because they are different from yours. People's individual experiences and frames of reference are big inhibitors. Most people seem only to relate to the reality they see and have personal experience in. For instance, when Bill Rosenzweig began to test the viability of his idea to start up the Republic of Tea, he began to appreciate how difficult a challenge he had taken on:

> My mind is full of my last conversation with Drake Sadler. It was the most discouraging conversation to date and the one it seems you always come to when you want to start something new.
>
> This was the conversation where you hear these kinds of things (coming from a person who is there and who has tried):
>
> 1. The market is controlled by several big players
> 2. There is little opportunity left
> 3. The field is not as hot as it was
> 4. There's a lot of people already doing it
> 5. Who needs another one
> 6. Difficult if not impossible to move within the market
> 7. Difficult if not impossible to enter mass market
> 8. Very risky to get involved
> 9. Nothing new to be done.
>
> In the bigger context, these are the types of things you always run into when you start a new business. I guess it means you are starting to be successful in your research— discovering the down side and risks as well as the potential. But this is the moment that separates entrepreneurs from weenies.

Engaging the will and spirit of your enterprise is a critical challenge and one which will largely determine whether or not your new idea will become a reality or remain a pipe dream. There are three major elements:

ENVISIONING

My friend Lou Gaviglia tells a story about a blind kid he knew growing up in his neighborhood. The kid started up a toy business that ultimately became a thriving enterprise. When people asked him how a blind kid could be so successful, he told them, "I may not be able to see, but that doesn't mean I lack vision."

Envisioning creates a compelling picture of ultimate possibility that allows you and others to see your innovative idea as a reality existing in time and space. Envisioning engages your creative unconscious allowing you to discover opportunities where none existed before. Through envisioning you imagine new possibilities into existence—and, when you involve your suppliers and customers in this process, you not only raise their awareness about exciting new possibilities for them, you also benefit from their wisdom about the kinds of products and services that will delight them. For instance, Marriott's chain of Courtyard hotels has adopted the slogan "Courtyard, the hotel designed by business travelers." They attribute their success to providing the services asked for by their customers. They purposefully used their customers as a vital source of knowledge about services that mattered to them. Each Courtyard employee is a highly skilled listener working in an environment designed to value and support the rapid transformation of knowledge gained in dialogue with customers into innovative ideas no other hotel has thought of. By the time their competition catches up, the idea is already old at Courtyard.

This is an important function of power partnering, because it changes our thinking from the realm of opportunity to the realm of possibility. The distinction is an important one; most companies are predisposed to the belief that they can only choose among a limited number of options or opportunities available to them. This limiting belief, based on the clock-logic assumption that we have our world all figured out, blinds us to the fact that there is a whole world of possibility out there that cannot be experienced based on history. As I have stressed throughout the first part of the book, we can't step outside of our experience and view the world from a privileged place of objectivity. No amount of looking hard will interrupt the flow of time long enough for us to see all our possibilities at once.

Power partnering is based on an entirely different set of assumptions about the way the world is perceived by us. From a power partnering perspective, we don't always know what we and our customers could aspire to without knowing what is possible. When we form power partnerships, we challenge ourselves and our customers to explore together innovative possibilities—not from our knowledge of the past, but from our mutual commitment to inventing the future. That doesn't mean we create our futures outside of experience—that would simply be a "pipe dream"—but we grasp possibilities as they come at us. When we envision we carry our future in the back of our mind and let our creative unconscious go to work. It is amazing how new possibilities suddenly appear where before none existed. People who are not aware of this process stumble over opportunities and dismiss them as mere coincidence, which they may well be. But when we deliberately seek out coincidences through envisioning, we make it possible to invent our future while our competitors are still reinventing their past.

MEMO

To: The Reader

From: Sean

Date: January 21st, 1996

Subject: A Long Walk in the Forest

My wife, Katherine, and I had, for the past few months, been reconsidering the vision we had created for our two companies. Originally we had seen them as two separate entities, but when we dug deeper, we realized that a thread connected them both. The thread became the word, "Teknowledging" and that, in turn, became the new name of our one company—Teknowledging, Inc. The only problem was, we didn't have a product, a knowledging technology.

So we created for ourselves a vision of what one might look like. One day, while we were walking in a beautiful Welsh forest, Katherine remembered talking to someone the previous week who knew someone who had developed a computer-based product that helped companies monitor the price of all goods they purchased. By setting up a knowledge network, the system allowed companies to share knowledge with one another about best purchasing practices. It was clear we had found our product (or more to the point, Pricetrak had found us); and when we eventually met its inventor, we were not surprised to learn that he was looking for someone to promote his product in the USA.

Sean

PLANNING

John Lennon said, "life is what happens when you are busy making other plans"—a point not wasted on Henry Mintzberg (1994), who makes the following point:

> Planning has become the articulation and elaboration of strategies, or visions, that already exist. When companies understand the difference between planning and strategic thinking, they can get back to what the strategy-making

process should be: capturing what the manager learns from all sources (both the soft insights from his or her personal experiences and the experiences of others throughout the organization and the hard data from market research and the like) and then synthesizing that learning into a vision of the direction that the business should pursue.

There is both a predictive and an emergent aspect to planning as we develop insights from the doing of our planning and integrate them into new plans. In other words, all planning is doing and all doing is planning. Likewise, power partnerships attempt to predict the future accurately while creating a future that was not going to happen otherwise—that is, a future that was not predictable. For instance, only weeks after an inventor's young daughter asked why she had to wait to see the picture he had just taken of her, Mintzberg tells us, "Edwin Land conceived the Polaroid camera, an invention that would transform his company. Land's vision was the synthesis of the insight evoked by his daughter's question and his vast technical knowledge."

Through practicing formal/informality, power partnerships use planning as a means of consciously doing and at the same time, unconsciously doing/not doing. In this way, they intentionally go after specific objectives while, equally intentionally, discerning the emerging patterns of possibility that come about specifically because they are up to something else. For instance, while looking for markets for Pricetrak, I became involved, for quite a different reason, with a health-care cooperative that leveraged price advantages for its members. While talking to people, a theme began to emerge about buying strategies. While some people felt that a single-source approach was easier and less complicated, others felt that multi-sourcing offered greater benefits because the competitive market forces would yield lower price advantages. When I asked the obvious question—"Why can't you do both?"—I was told that tracking and controlling the data was virtually impossible with so many line items and so many vendors.

I was able to show them that it was not only possible, but that I just happened to own the product that would allow them to do that. The reason they had not found me earlier was that they believed the problem was *virtually* impossible, an unfortunate slip of the tongue that blinded them to a *real* possibility. All it takes is prepared minds and happy accidents to invent a future that would not happen otherwise. Opportunities are what happen while you are doing other plans.

Envisioning raises more possibilities than you could ever hope to convert into products and services at any one time. Consequently, scoping allows you to reflect on your mission, values, and vision, and then to use these as criteria to determine which opportunities to pursue immediately, which to pursue later, and which to leave alone or pass along to a competitor. For example, in our story about CFC elimination, the computer company gave the patents to another company because they were not in the business of making cleaning equipment.

Once identified, innovative ideas have to be transformed into real products and services. This is the juncture at which more formal plans are required. For example, Bill Rosenzweig, CEO of the Republic of Tea, created short-term goals covering the first eighteen months of the business:

> During the first 18 months of operation, our goal is to establish prominent national distribution and create a highly visible product and brand identity that exemplifies the quality and aesthetic of the business.

and longer-term goals (eighteen months to three years), like the following:

> Expand the company's product line, exploring specialty food extensions such as cookies, cakes, bottled beverages. Also explore further extensions of the brand to include lifestyle opportunities like clothing, furnishings, and housewares. Explore the potential to license designs and the TRoT brand identity to other leading manufacturers.

The planning phase is an opportunity to manage the inevitable tension between the practical day to day doing and the insightful and creative process of doing/not doing. Power partnering requires mastery in managing the tension between both. Forcing anything makes it part of whatever it is you are creating—and, as Mel Ziegler, one of the founders of the Republic of Tea, has said, forcing something into existence will one day lead to its undoing:

> In conceiving and brainstorming and imagining the Republic of Tea, none of us wanted to force something that did not want to be—concepts, structures, relationships. Difficult as it was for us at times, we learned to listen to it. This is our proudest achievement. Whether it translates to a huge business success remains to be seen. Only time will tell if there were lapses in our awareness that also resulted in an unwillingness to listen to, or an unwillingness to see something about the business, about ourselves, about the relationships. If there were, these, too, will be part of the business and we will pay the consequences for them later.

Successful power partnerships are made up of people who are committed to and who engage the commitment of others, to build a future that would not happen otherwise. They articulate this commitment in conversations for possibility where a future gets created in the speaking of the partners. Once a future has been created in a conversation for possibility, the resources of an organization and the reality with which it must deal begin to show up differently for people. They begin to see new ways to employ the resources and new openings in the reality. They manage the context of their journey by constantly reminding themselves and others about the purpose of the mission and their commitment to its success.

COMMITTING

Benjamin Franklin said, "well done is better than well said." While it is true that some people have a flare for thinking and some for acting, power partnering requires skill in both domains. I have seen many partnerships brought to their knees by a lack of willingness to act on the part of their members.

This unwillingness usually shows up as a predisposition for data gathering and analysis. Like an expensive sports car with no transmission, the sleek, highly precise idea cannot move into action because conversations among the partners never move beyond description and explanation. The worst kind of inaction is the famous "rock fetching" exercise where people are sent of in all direction to collect data that will never be the right kind. The plan is to delay as long as you can so you keep asking for more data—which, of course, isn't what you asked for, so you send people off again, and so on without end. The game can go on for an awful long time—at least until the information-gatherers refuse to do it any more.

Another strong indicator of a person's unwillingness to act shows up in her or his speaking. Characteristic statements of such unwillingness are "I guess we ought to go ahead," or "That seems like a good idea—I'll think about it," or "I think maybe we should call them. I'll try to do it by next week." It is this uncommitted speaking that absolutely kills any chance of innovative ideas moving into action, no matter how brilliant they are. Without this commitment to action, spoken by people, no-thing happens. This kind of "cheap talk" is incredibly expensive when it prevents or severely delays the bringing of leading-edge products and services to your marketplace. It simply cannot be tolerated in power partnerships where time is of the essence and people depend heavily on one another to do what they say they will do. Power partnering places special emphasis on the language of action—and especially the committed speaking and listening that is essential to excellent coordination of action. Committing is about "buying into" the challenge of the mission and committing to moving beyond talk and into action.

Committing assigns actual capabilities to the various teams. Through a process of multiplexing, people in your enterprise will participate on one or more power partnerships at any one time, yielding a constant and continual interfeeding of ideas. This networks the organization in an organic way.

Committing is gaining personal commitment to the mission and values of the teams. In power partnerships people speak and act from their shared commitment to a future they have yet to make happen. The bigger the challenge, the bigger the commitment—because the temptation to give up at the first hurdle is extremely strong. It is essential that all those people who will play a significant part in the success of the mission be involved in its creation.

10

Creating:
Building Communities of Knowledge

When we attempt to start up a new project, we begin by putting in place the appropriate structure. We then create systems to put routine and order into the organization. Having done that, we then leave people to figure out for themselves how to get around these constraints in order to work together.

Power partnerships do the opposite. They build systems and structures that enable and encourage the social interaction required to perform work effectively and efficiently. Power partnerships operate in environments that enable and encourage co-workers and people from different departments and disciplines to listen insightfully to one another, imagine new possibilities, and design them into being. Consider, for example, the text of Lotus Development Corporation's recent advertisement in the British Sunday Times:

> There's more to British Aerospace than making an 85,000-lb piece of metal fly like a bird. Freedom on the ground is just as important.

Now, with the help of Lotus Notes, British Aerospace soars to even greater heights. Information passes freely from site to site and ideas move quicker. From the person on the ground all the way up to the director of the board.

Now collaboration improves as teams become more effective. Sharing knowledge, minute by minute, day by day.

Helping to keep British Aerospace up there.

The Power of Notes is the power of shared knowledge.

Likewise, the power of power partnering is the power of shared knowledge; its outcome is continuous innovating leading to outstandingly original products and services. Creating is about building environments that trigger interaction among individuals, and promote new ways of thinking and fresh ideas. In these environments, people use information to leverage and share knowledge on an as-needed basis. They are not overloaded with useless information but enriched by relevant information that helps them solve business problems and seek out new opportunities. These environments increase the flow of transformative energy that brings to life the images generated during the imagining process. Such environments enable the flow of innovative ideas throughout the entire organization, making them available to all people wherever and whenever required. They also create real-time, standard practices, such as engineering design specifications, so that up-to-date knowledge may be shared with other teams performing similar tasks. The last thing you need is to invent the wheel five times in any one week.

Power partnering environments are stagile—having the stability to produce high-quality products and services routinely while being willing and able to integrate new ideas quickly. They provide an environment in which networks of conversations leading to the creation of innovative ideas can take place—and where conversations hinging on requests and promises transform these ideas into action. Using groupware (such as Lotus Notes or Microsoft Exchange) and physically changing the workspace in ways that bring people together instead of keeping them apart, power partnering environments allow you to leverage the incremental innovation coming from within your entire company.

Take, for example, IDEO Product Development, one of the world's most celebrated design firms. David Kelley, IDEO's founder, describes his company as "a living laboratory of the workplace. The company is in a state of perpetual experimentation, where we are constantly trying out new ideas in our projects, our work space, and our culture." Tia O'Brian's recent article in *Fast Company* magazine describes IDEO in the following way:

> Kelley is adamant that people can't be creative without heavy doses of freedom and fun. There are no bosses or job titles. All work is organized into project teams that form and disband in a matter of weeks or months. There are no permanent job assignments; designers are free to move to Chicago or Tokyo if they can find a colleague willing to switch.

Kelley will tell you the most important thing he learned from big companies is that creativity gets stifled when everyone has to follow the rules. This doesn't mean that the people at IDEO are unaccountable for their actions; on the contrary, these principles are an earnest attempt to create radical new ideas that become important new products. Kelley says, "the primary engine for innovation at IDEO is its distinct approach to brainstorming. It is the only part of the company where strict rules do apply." According to O'Brian, sessions are held in specially designated "brainstormer rooms" where participants can draw almost anywhere: on whiteboard-covered walls, on conference tables covered with paper. In addition, multimedia tools, like televisions, VCRs, and computer projectors, are used to enhance the creative process.

These sessions usually happen at the aspiring stage of a project, when people from a range of disciplines are invited. Although informal in nature, the rules of brainstorming are taken seriously:

1. Stay focused on your purpose
2. Encourage wild ideas
3. Defer judgment
4. Build on the ideas of others
5. One conversation at a time.

According to O'Brian, "promising ideas are quickly transformed into foam or cardboard models and as they become more robust, they go to the company's machine shop where powerful computer-controlled machine tools generate prototypes from plastic or metal within hours of receiving software files from a designer's computer."

Creating work environments where improvisations can be captured and made part of your organization's collective knowledge base requires a fundamental understanding and mapping of the material and information flows required to support the commitments you have made. It requires that you make these flows and their relationship to one another visible to all participants. Key to this process is your ability to get back to basics by creating and maintaining an organizational context that is founded on your core purpose and operating philosophy, and then putting in place the people networks and technical processes, systems, and structures necessary to enable outstanding coordination of action. The result is a work environment that embraces both routine and non-routine activities—an environment in which, instead of either/or thinking, you can adopt a both/and approach to working with both the parts and the whole system, ensuring the skillful and seamless transformation of opportunities (raised in the non-routine domain) into mass-customized products and services. Moreover, when patterns are discovered in the non-routine domain, you will flow them into the routine domain through the discipline of mass customization. As John Seeley Brown (1991) points out:

The trend towards mass customization is made possible by technology. The emphasis, however, is not on the technology itself but on the work practices it supports. In the future, organizations won't have to shape how they work to fit the narrow confines of an inflexible technology. Rather, they begin to design information systems to support the way people really work.

11

Transforming:
Shaping Innovative Ideas into Real Products and Services

Transforming is about executing your plans and maintaining an appreciation for the uniqueness and direction of your enterprise as people work together to make the dream a reality. It is about transforming ideas into products and services while, at the same time, becoming transformed by the reflexive and reflective insights ensuing from those actions. There are two stages:

IMPLEMENTING

Implementing is concerned with producing the products and services that delight your customers. It is about remaining committed to your highest aspirations and staying true to your core values. Implementing means sticking to your plans and dealing with the unforeseen consequences of your actions. It is about observing and reflecting upon those consequences, and developing new insights that become the life blood of your organization by providing the knowledge that enhances your capacity to innovate. In a culture of valuing, people "pull" on this knowledge as they interact with each other in mutually dependent ways, continually seeking out the patterns of meaning in events as they unfold. In support of the core purpose, they combine their knowledge and strengths with others to leverage more opportunities. Implementing in this way makes it possible for you to achieve much more than you had imagined, both individually and within and between functions and companies.

Power partnering requires an entirely new mindset about information, knowledge, and the way people learn. In power partnerships the emphasis is on action and improvement; direct and real learning that serves both individual and organizational requirements and leads to capability in action and creativity in thinking is encouraged. As Brook Manville and Nathaniel Foote (1996) put it:

> Knowledge-based strategies should emphasize on-the-job learning rather than traditional training. "Just in time" learning which takes place in the moment of actual need not only creates the most value; it also makes the biggest impression on the learner and the organization. Ultimately, learning is up to each individual—it's not something that management can require. The essence of successful knowledge-based strategies is a company's capacity to raise the aspirations of each employee. These are the people whose contributions and ongoing development become the lifeblood of performance gains.

Power partnerships regard learning, whether personal or organizational, as a process within life and within whatever you are doing. It is a process that centers on becoming increasingly perceptive about the patterns that connect you with others and your world. It requires a deep understanding of your feelings and values, and a belief that you have choice about the direction of your life. Power partnering is a journey along a path that broadens and deepens your understanding of yourself, the aspirations and capabilities of others, and what they cause to happen in the world. The essence of your learning is your capacity to become willful about your learning and mindful of what is happening around and within you.

Fulfilling your organization's potential is a continual process of learning from your attempts to fill the voids created when your aspirations exceed your abilities. Organizational learning is a consequence of your willingness to exchange the lenses through which you view and make sense of the world and, with your new lenses, to open up to the new possibilities that come into view. Likewise, work is about filling voids and improving the value of things. Power partnering encourages immediate, direct, and real learning that serves both your personal and organizational aspirations. It leads to capability in action and creativity and innovation in thinking and learning.

Power partnering further meets your needs to increase your capacity to develop new skills and awareness continually, and provides the opportunity and the tools for self-motivation and self-empowerment. Power partnering emphasizes continuous learning, teaming, and redefining structure to take advantage of ever-changing opportunities. Power partnerships create leading-edge products and services routinely, while seizing and capitalizing on new possibilities as they appear in their marketplace.

APPRECIATING

Probably the most critical ingredient in the process of transforming innovative ideas into leading-edge services and products is that of maintaining appreciation for your organizational context—that mix of aspiration, vision, and values which together forms your master plan for building a culture of unity and innovation. For want of a better word, I call this leading. When I say leading, I don't mean the old style of exerting "power over and control of" people; instead, I mean leadership as an interpretive process. As Gareth Morgan and Linda Smircich put it, leadership is "maintaining the actions and utterances which, consciously and unconsciously, shape the meaning of situations and guide the attention of those involved." The old style of leadership supported the belief that people, like other resources, had to be controlled in order to produce the product. Power partnerships, on the other hand, are about forming dynamic relationships of knowledge interaction and exchange, leading to powerful synergies of insight. These cannot be controlled; they must be nurtured.

Maintaining appreciation in this way makes it easier for people to align and re-align their talents dynamically and in meaningful ways that produce innovative ideas. Consequently, appreciating involves your continual reflecting on the context of your work and maintaining alignment among your actions within that context. In the course of my own research on the characteristics of power partnerships, people have told me that leadership and learnership are key ingredients to success. "You must have somebody who keeps announcing what the expectation is," one person told me. "Influencing people to adopt a particular course of action," say others. "Focusing attention on the status of specific goals." "Engaging people in conversations about end points and holding them accountable for their promises to achieve them." "Developing trust and commitment." "Creating possibilities." "Generating requests and promises." The list goes on, but the common thread running throughout is that leadership is the act of creating and maintaining meaning.

The old notion of leaders as "Great Men" who derived their power through withholding or selectively leaking out information is fast being replaced by a generation of leaders who inspire people through their ability to freely share information in ways that bring meaning into people's lives. Their mastery lies in their ability to provide information that becomes, in Gregory Bateson's words, the "difference that makes the difference." When information performs this role, it is no longer information but knowledge—and knowledge is power. Good leaders create environments where people are at liberty to use their fullest potential in powerful ways. In power-partnering environments, people and the organizations they form become enriched in a way that moves both a step closer to fulfilling their potential. Both become more knowledgeable.

MEMO

To: The Reader

From: Sean

Date: March 9th, 1996

Subject: A View of Today's Reinvented Manager

If you think we don't have a challenge developing managers who can lead power partnerships, the following survey, carried out by Stephen Kauffman for the *Boston Business Journal*, might convince you otherwise. According to Kauffman, the top ten concerns people share about their managers are:

1. Out of touch: There is no nicer way of referring to the boss who is ineffectual. These are the supervisors who know less than their subordinates and lack the understanding about what the people underneath them are actually doing. Also included in this category are managers who are unaware of destructive rivalries among employees.

2. Too many missions and directions: With only so many hours in the week, this was one of the most frequent complaints of employees. It is one thing to manage in times of uncertainty, but when this spills over into a stream of inconsistent instructions, not only is energy sapped but enthusiasm and employee belief is lowered.

3. Not sharing information: Proof that the old belief, control of information equals power, is still alive. Unfortunately, for the believers in the age of information, it is speed of dissemination that counts. How else can people do their jobs and meet or exceed the benchmark standards?

4. Steal the work of employees: The consequences of stealing are worse than the demoralizing effects it has on its victim. It hurts you as well, because your company loses twice. First, the knowledge of who has the actual talent remains hidden. Second, when a manager steals the credit for someone's work, as case histories show, it is not long before the real inventor leaves the company.

5. Engaging in illegal activities: This evil still makes the top ten list. The specifics of the acts, however, are defined by a multitude of ills such as: embezzlement, sexual harass-ment, deceptive marketing, billing fraud, labor infractions, product alterations, and falsification of information. When employees observe managers engaging in such practices, a tarnish spreads across the entire company.

6. Sabotaging company objectives for the sake of a personal goal: Whether altered goals occur as a territorial conquest of another department or is founded on the ego or income gratification needs of the boss, the results are the same. Employees are asked to serve dual masters. Allowed to go unchecked, it will not be long before your employees are working towards ends not defined by you.

7. Living by different standards: The "do as I say" mantra preached by managers who do as they please is the most irksome and frequent complaint of employees. While not the greatest sin in the top 10, it becomes fuel to feed employee anger and discontent. The double standard breeds a sense of unfairness that leads to cynicism and lack of loyalty.

8. Not using authority: The greatest way to lose power is to not use it. Employees describe how they become the brunt of such weakness when the boss, for example, does not take charge, fails to defend staff or decisions, shifts responsibility to avoid blame and allows bickering to exist.

9. Setting objectives that cannot be met: There is a difference between a challenging goal and a task doomed to failure. The former exhilarates and bonds the work force; the latter demoralizes and destroys vitality and incentive. What is the distinction between the two? In the doomed category, the boss makes commitment to please others, even when she or he knows it can't be reached. In the challenge group, a leader is driven by a vision and works harder than anyone to reach it. Employees still follow leaders.

10. Assuming familiarity with subordinates: Managers have a great power over the lives and fortunes of those under them. Taking advantage of that authority with casual jokes, inquiries into private lives, and asking for personal favors is seen by employees as intrusive. The numbers are larger than you

think, but because of the fear of reprisal, workers hide their true feelings.

Sean

In power partnerships, leading is a process rather than a person. As such, the function of leadership can be performed by an individual or a group of individuals. Understanding leading from this perspective helps in focusing your efforts, not on managing and controlling people, but on maintaining appreciation for your aspirations through creating and maintaining meaning. As one manager told me: "Everyone knows what they have to do to satisfy the customer and make the business a success. My job is to let people get on with their work uninterrupted and to manage the noise at the interface between my organization and its environment."

When you lead in this way, you display an ability to interpret what is going on around you, and to understand both the conversations in which you participate and the identity you create for yourself within them. You expand your capacity to listen to how others listen to you. You have a clear sense of who you are because you understand the history into which you were born, the history you have created for yourself, and how both set your horizon of possibility. Leading through appreciating means you are skilled at reflecting-on-action and at reflexing-in-action, because you use both ways of knowing to grasp what is happening around you.

Part 3

Power Partnering Applications

This third part of *Power Partnering* is concerned with the application of the ideas presented in the previous chapters within your organization. In this section we will take a look at some of the key factors to be taken into consideration before implementing a power partnering strategy in your organization. For instance, should you appoint a dedicated person responsible for implementing your strategy? If so, who should that person be? How do you implement a power partnering strategy so that people feel committed to its success? What is the most effective way to develop people's capability to lead, manage, and participate in power partnerships? How will this be done? There is the need to recognize which power-partnering "teknowledgy" will apply in which particular situation. Finally, how should effective power partnerships be recognized and rewarded?

There is no quick and easy solution that fits all contexts and needs. What worked in one situation may not work in another, and the success of any application will depend on the committed and coordinated effort of all those people involved. One important point to remember, however, is that becoming a power-partnering enterprise is not as easy as it may seem to those who believe that an occasional meeting with the customer, or a purposing session with a team, is what its all about. Unless implementation is handled effectively, power partnering can become a sort of peripheral luxury that has little relevance to the success of your organization.

In a new economy that is fast recognizing the value of a company's knowledge assets, power partnering is of serious importance—an importance that can only grow in the future. There is a need for power partnering, and for the continual discovery of effective ways to introduce it into organizations. The time has never been more suited, or the need more pressing.

12

Serious and Day-to-Day Power Partnering

To make the distinction between serious and day-to-day power partnering, it might be helpful to think of the levels of energy or degrees of effort required to transform your innovative ideas into leading-edge products and services (see Figure 12–1). John Bennett put forward the notion that there are universal energies organized into levels according to their degree of structure. According to Bennett, the most basic form of human energy is automatic energy; this is energy that keeps things going without any act of attention or anything that requires you to be directly aware of anything. Those of you who have driven home from work along your regular route without having to think consciously of the route will know what automatic energy is. At a higher level, we get into the realm of sensitive energy, which requires more attention because it involves awareness. There is very little awareness at the automatic level, even though information can be taken in and dealt with in an efficient way. With sensitivity, we become aware of our surroundings. While on your routine drive home from work, you might become sensitive to a sound coming from your engine and the smell of something burning.

At the next level we enter the domain of consciousness, a much higher level of awareness that brings meaning to our sensing. You pull over to the side of the road and lift up the hood of your car. To your surprise, you notice you have lost coolant from your engine. At the next level we enter the realm of creative energy associated with spontaneity, in that it requires our doing/not doing in order to be effective. You are totally unprepared for this breakdown and moreover, you don't know the first thing about replacing the coolant in your car. You read your maintenance manual and learn how to do what needs to be done; but you have no water and, even if you did, you have nothing to carry it in. In any case, even if you had both it wouldn't help, because you have a slow leak in your radiator.

You look around and find that the road you are on runs by a golf course and there, right next to the tee, is a drinking water fountain. You dig around in the undergrowth by the roadside and find a discarded beer can. Further investigation of the road surface turns up an old piece of chewing gum. Before you know it, you are back on the road again, having creatively used materials that were not previously intended for the use you put them to. Day-to-day power partnering typically falls into this range of progressively increasing levels of energy that drive automatic, sensing, conscious, and creative modes of thinking.

Serious power partnering takes day-to-day energy to substantially higher levels. Going beyond the creative level of energy we come to unitive energy, which is the power to engage the collective will of many people and unite them around a common cause. An example of unitive energy is what happened after Ray Kroc had to get creative in order to find a conveniently located, inexpensive, high-quality restaurant while on a long journey with his family. Having failed in his search, Kroc didn't stop there. He invented McDonald's so that other people would never have to go through the inconvenience he had been through. In order to make his dream a reality, Kroc realized he needed the help of other people—people who would lend him money, build his restaurants, service his customers, and market his services and products. In short, he badly needed people who would share his dream. His challenge was to infuse others with his will and spirit. He had to help them see his vision in the way he saw it. This is the power of unitive energy, the power to engage people in the relentless pursuit of a shared vision. However, in order to achieve lasting change, we need the ultimate level of energy—one that makes McDonald's so natural a way of life that a McDonaldless world becomes unthinkable.

The energy I am talking about is transcendent energy, the power to change the way the world thinks. One of the best descriptions I have read on the power of transcendent energy is that provided by the late Lancelot Whyte, who believed that great steps in human history are anticipated and probably brought about by changes in the unconscious thinking of thousands and millions of individuals during the period preceding the change. Then, in a relatively short space of time, a new idea, a new perspective, seems to burst upon the world scene—and change occurs.

In order to create transformations we require not only a transcendent level of energy; we must exercise as well a transforming mode of thinking to maintain alignment between unitive and transcendent energies. Once in the domain of transcendent energy, our transforming mode of thinking makes ordinary and routine what we once regarded as innovative. These new patterns are integrated into our existing patterns and become automatic at a higher level of awareness, thereby initiating a new cycle of energy. This is what it means to be human, to be constantly seeking to fulfill our true potential. In other words, as the late Carl Rogers (1980) pointed out:

> Organisms are always seeking, always initiating, always "up
> to something." There is usually in any new development, a
> subterranean current in the popular mind and feeling, which
> grows stronger and stronger until, with a seeming
> suddenness, it breaks forth into clearly articulated form in

various places and countries. In this sense I believe there is, alongside the obviously destructive forces on our planet, a growing current that will lead to a new level of human awareness.

Those who witnessed the destruction of the Berlin Wall will attest to this phenomenon. In time, the wall will no longer appear to have been real to people. The wall will exist in the pages of history books where the context behind its destruction will be lost to subsequent generations. This is the challenge of implementing power partnerships on a serious basis. You are, in essence, breaking down the Berlin Walls inside your organizations, allowing the free and unhampered energy of innovating to occur through knowledge networking. After all, its what we humans do quite naturally in spite of the barriers imposed by machine-age clock logic. The process of day-to-day and serious power partnering might be depicted in the following way:

DAY-TO-DAY POWER PARTNERING

The teknowledgies outlined in this section can be used in everyday situations that require creative reflection and insightful action. However, these situations do not require any formal or deliberate effort. They can happen whenever and wherever there is a willingness to look for new ideas and to value and build on the ideas of others.

Declaring a Crisis

This is the willingness to declare a crisis when everything is running smoothly. Asking questions like "what if?" and "why not?" interrupt the smooth flow of ordinary life and create space for new insights and possibilities to emerge. For instance, Galileo declared a crisis when he challenged the Ptolemic theory of an earth-centered universe. When Akio Morita, the chairman of Sony, was told by his market research people that

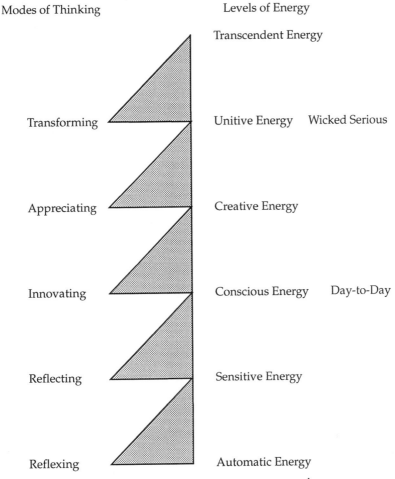

Figure 12-1   Creating Power Partnerships

consumers wouldn't buy a tape recorder that wouldn't record, he built the Sony Walkman anyway. Once you declare a new world into existence, you make possible the opportunity to invent a new future that simply would not happen otherwise. Once Columbus proved the earth was round, people were free to explore all kinds of possibilities once deemed unimaginable. What "flat earth thinking" is keeping you attached to "clock logic" notions of organizing? What have you allowed yourself to become comfortable with? What innovative ideas and creative solutions are being suppressed by management systems that exercise power over and control of people? What is the cost of devaluing and distrust in your organization?

Stagility

Here, we are referring to the willingness to think "outside of the box" when it comes to receiving a request from a customer that doesn't fit the normal pattern of doing things. I recently phoned for technical assistance after my computer broke down. After holding on the line for over an hour, I was eventually connected to a technician who told me exactly what to do; before I could try out his advice, he hung up on me. I did as instructed and my computer still didn't work. I called again and after another hour, was connected to a different technician who told me what to do. I insisted that he stay on the line while I put his advice into action, and he reluctantly agreed. I did what he said and proceeded to wipe my hard disk completely clean. When I told him I had lost all my files, he told me it was my problem because I should have backing up my data and hung up the phone. I called a third time; one hour later, I found myself talking with B.K. Patel. He didn't work in that department, but had volunteered to help out because they were overloaded with calls.

Like all the others, B.K. could not fix the problem, but unlike all the others, he said he would. He gave me his personal telephone and fax numbers and asked me to fax him specific information on my machine. He worked through his lunch break and, after seeking the advice of engineers who had designed my model of computer, he called me back and together we fixed my problem. After thanking him profusely, he told me I would probably be the only person to do so. He went on to tell me that technicians in his company are rewarded for the speed in which they solve problems. Since he had spent the best part of half a day solving my problem and cost his company a two-hour long-distance telephone call, he wasn't looking for accolades. I wrote to his supervisor letting her know that, if it weren't for B.K., I would not be buying a second computer from them. His ability to become agile while working within the stable confines of the technical repair system got them a delighted customer and one who would buy their products again. (B.K. if you are reading this book, thanks again!)

Both/And Thinking

This teknowledgy is nothing more or less than the willingness to remove "versus" from your conversations. It requires a quality of listening and speaking that connects the dichotomies created in language. For instance, both/and thinking is essential in situations in which production is accusing design of not involving them in the development of new products. Production people think that designers throw new products "over the wall" and then expect them to build them. These situations are ideal for both/and thinking because they allow both sides of an argument to begin a dialogue that will lead to solutions integrating *both* design *and* production. By shifting your fixed patterns of thinking, you make new possibilities happen. There is a well-known problem in the plastic and paper bag industry. Those who make paper bags would like to produce them at the price of a plastic bag. Those who use them love the fact that they stand up when you fill them. Those in the plastic bag industry are trying to make a plastic bag that stands up like a paper bag, but costs the same as a plastic bag. A both/and solution might be the paper "handbag"—a bag having a bottom half made out of paper so it stands up, and a top half made from plastic with handles for strength, ease of carrying, and (above all) low cost.

Listening

Listening is, as we have said earlier, the willingness to turn down your inner conversation in order to hear others. In a world of TV sets where everyone transmits and few receive, listening is a valuable strategy for understanding the discourse behind the noise. When asked to help resolve a conflict between individuals, teams, or entire organizations, one of my most favorite tactics is a very simple listening practice. Before bringing the differing parties together, I spend time with each, gathering the following information:

1. What do you value about your relationship with the other/s?
2. What's missing from your relationship with the other/s?
3. What do you think the other/s will have on their list?

I invite the differing parties to come together to review the lists. A representative from each side presents the three lists, which are then posted on the wall on large sheets of paper. Only questions for clarification are allowed. In nearly all cases, what appeared to be an insurmountable rift between them comes down to a small handful of issues around which action plans for resolution are created.

While I call this process listening, there will be times when the issues are simply too complex to discern patterns through auditory means alone. In these cases it becomes necessary to engage, what my friend Russ Doane (1995) calls "eye muscle empowerment":

> When I hear complexity bogging down discussion, I look around for a way people can use their eyes to abstract and display some of what they are struggling with. For example, while listening to a welfare expert speak, I made a crude cause-and effect-diagram showing many wellsprings and

tributaries by which people flood into welfare. The complexity was then obvious to everyone who saw my sketch.

According to Russ (1995), our eyes work with shapes. With visual abstractions, we are not limited to a serial stream. At a glance, we can comprehend a shape as a whole. Moreover, many pairs of eyes in a team effort can randomly access any part of a visual display. Moreover, they can do so without mutual interference. Acoustic sounds interfere. In a meeting room, all users are obliged to treat their common sound field as a scarcity:

> *Don't interrupt, Quiet please, She has the floor, Order!* But there is no need for order when all eyes are independent. Each person brings their own selective glancing. Any number of people are free to see what they choose to look at. Many independently-focusing eyes give a large group many times more freedom. This is why "on-the-wall" meetings—made possible by the development of flip-chart paper and 3M's Post-It Notes and its clones—are so powerful.

Valuing

After spending 932 days together circumnavigating the earth, Bill Fallon, Tim Sperry, Chris Smith, Matt Sperry, and Mark Parsons, the crew of the sailing ketch *Lazarus*, said that their greatest achievement wasn't circling the globe but learning mutual tolerance. "We learned there are sometimes five right ways to solve a problem," said Mark Parsons. "Tolerance comes in learning sometimes to be quiet." The one thing they all agreed they would take with them for the rest of their lives was trust in each other.

While its not always possible, or desirable, to create an atmosphere of valuing in your power partnerships by undergoing some life-threatening experience, it is possible to do it by design. When setting up your power partnerships it is important to select people who value valuing and can provide evidence to this effect. Time must be spent building mutual valuing and commitment, in circumstances in which people keep their egos in check or at least declare when they are activated. Members of power partnerships are willing to self-disclose and declare a crisis. They are willing to ask and respond to questions. They are trusting and confident in the partnership's ability to achieve its aspirations. They defer their judgments and, in so doing, learn the judgments of others—and consequently, their own.

Building a valuing environment in power partnerships is best achieved through a process loosely based on George Kelly's theory of personal constructs. Basically, Kelly believed that people behave like scientists, exploring their environment. On the basis of these explorations, people construct their own individual maps of the world about them. They then use these maps to guide their actions. The valuing process is a way of surfacing individual maps and then looking for areas of overlap. You will be amazed at the level of commonality that can be achieved.

The process goes something like this: Think of six people who have made a significant impression in your life (you can build this around whatever theme is relevant to your purposes). Using six three-by-five-inch index cards, write one of the names on each of the six cards. Shuffle the cards and number them E1 through E6. Deal out cards E1, E2, E3, and think about each of these people in turn. Try to imagine yourself back in the situation with each of them in turn to rekindle your memory of them. Now think of them as impressive people. What was it they did that left such an impression on your life? Now ask yourself the question, which two people out of the three are most alike and which person is most unlike the other two? Put the two similar cards together and separate the third.

Using differently colored three-by-five card, label it C1P1 and write on it a brief description of what it is about the pair that leads you to group them together. When you have done this, label a second card C1P2 and write on it a brief description of what it is about the third person that makes that person different.

Put the C1P2 and C1P1 descriptions aside, deal out cards E4, E5, and E6, and repeat the procedure. Which two are most alike, and which one is different from the pair? Write a description of the similarity between the new pair on a card labeled C2P1 and a description of what separates the third person on a card labeled C2P2. Deal out cards E1, E3, and E5, and repeat the process creating two new cards labeled C3P1 and C3P2. Finally deal out E2, E4, and E6, and repeat the process creating two new cards labeled C4P1 and C4P2.

These construct cards are not just telling you something about the people you have named on your element cards E1 through E6; they are telling you something about yourself. They display some of the ways in which you think and feel about impressive people. Did you realize that you thought and felt that way about these people? If the activity gave you some clues to the way you think about impressive people in general, you may wish to repeat this activity in more depth with the people you already chose or include six others.

The power of this process, when applied to a newly formed (or about to be formed) power partnership, is that it allows each of you to know more about yourself and about the people you are about to partner with. In most cases, there will be many similarities and overlaps in values. Often you will discover amazing qualities in people. Sometimes you will find you have nothing in common, or worse still, feel unable to value the other people and decide to leave the partnership. Valuing in this way leads to more open and creative partnerships.

Envisioning

There have been more books, videos, courses, and audio cassettes on the subject of envisioning than you can poke a stick at. Based on your specific need, they all do a pretty good job. Personally speaking, I have a preference for the visual method of "eye muscle empowerment" that allows lots of participation and can be shared among large numbers of people. While there are new technologies that allow you to do computer visuals, I find there is nothing better than the good old-fashioned collage method for hands-on participation where people can literally see what you are talking about.

Using a collage, you can articulate your vision—or invite participation to create one with you—through placing pictures extracted from favorite magazines, catalogues, posters, and other sources on a large sheet of paper. The pictures are arranged in relationship to one another; and once you have reached agreement on their relative positions, you glue them in place. You can then photograph your collage and produce colorful posters that you can hang on your walls as a constant reminder of your vision and direction. Each of the images conveys a special meaning; if it were ever possible to put them on a computer, you would simply double-click on each image to be linked to serious plans, strategies with time lines, and performance measures.

In the rare situations in which where people cannot or do not wish to engage in such "childlike behavior" (as one senior executive characterized it to me), you might wish to engage the support of a skilled designer, one who can listen to your conversations and create the collage for you as you speak. For example, David Sibbet, the president and CEO of The Grove Consultants International, a strategic visioning and process consulting firm based in San Francisco, helped one company develop its vision:

> In the case of Merix, I listened to the discussion at a company retreat and tried to map out what I heard. The people were focused intensely on the company's core competencies and values. That was what they wanted to build around. The metaphor of space emerged. Merix sees itself not only as a high-tech company, but also as futuristic, a company going where no one has gone, on the leading edge of technology. So the design used the M logo as a spaceship. And the company's worldview, its global consciousness kept coming up. At the meeting, people

talked about how fast their industry moves and how dynamic and complex the business is. There were a few other key elements that had to be front and center: the importance of human resources, technology and their relationships with suppliers and customers.

The one distinctive feature of the Merix vision was the use of computer graphics as well as hand-written words. The company felt this conveyed both the business Merix is in, the space metaphor and their valuing of people.

Serious Power Partnering

The challenge of Serious Power Partnering is showing up to the people who are essential to your success, in a way that captures their imagination. As I have said all along, this is not easy: They will have difficulty seeing the challenge and the solution, and conceptualizing your innovative ideas, in the same way you do. Their mental picture of your challenge and their mental picture of your solution almost always mismatch because theirs are different from yours. People's individual experiences and frames of reference are big inhibitors. Most people seem only to relate to the reality they see and have personal experience with. So how do you prepare people so that it occurs to them that something really important is missing in their lives?

RAISING AWARENESS

Your aim is to have power partnering be a natural part of your organization's culture. But, as with all things, before a new world can occur naturally to people, they must first declare themselves willing listeners and beginners in that new domain. Only then will they be open to experiencing its possibilities for themselves, and willing to begin a process of wobbling with the concepts until they become second nature. Awakening the senses is best achieved with in-house seminars delivered to senior managers. Such seminars should not be restricted to certain groups of executives, but to representatives from across your organization. If your CEO and top management take a direct and personal interest in power partnering, then the practice stands an excellent chance of spreading very rapidly throughout your company. The key to successful power partnering is a demonstrated commitment, on behalf of senior managers, to creating an environment that values innovation through power partnering. When this commitment becomes reflected in their actions, success is guaranteed. One way you can do this is by appointing a vice president of power partnering and innovation or, like the people at Steelcase, a vice president of technical discovery and innovation.

Another important way of ensuring success is to demonstrate your commitment to innovating through power partnering, by establishing cultural artifacts that reflect your aspirations and espoused values. John Bennett proposed four key dimensions of culture:

1. Status: What you, as an organization, view as important.
2. Totems: The symbols of success you associate with that status.
3. Rituals: Recurring events, ceremonial acts, formal events you perform to celebrate conformance to the values of your organization.
4. Taboos: The things you remove or disallow.

A good example of these four dimensions can be seen on your television screen once a year. The Masters' golf championship is held every year at the Augusta National Golf Club in Augusta, Georgia. For the past sixty-two years Augusta National has hosted this prestigious golfing event, and evidence of the four dimensions of culture are present wherever you look. Firstly, there is great status afforded those golfers who have attained outstanding levels of mastery in the sport of golf. The symbols of success are reflected in the clothes they wear, the equipment they use, the green jackets worn only by those who have won the Masters, the trophies and money awards presented to the winners, the photographs and plaques displayed on the walls, even the television flashbacks to their moments of greatness. The ritual is the Masters championship itself; its regular occurrence each year and the celebrations surrounding the event. The taboos are displayed in the many rules of etiquette such as dress codes for golfers, caddies, officials, and spectators. They are also embodied in the rules of golf that constitute fair play and that, if breached, will lead to immediate expulsion from the tournament.

How might you use these dimensions to establish the kind of culture that reflects your aspirations and values? What is the relationship between all four that forms the essence of your culture—the context out of which you act? If you say you give status to innovating through power partnering yet have no rituals, totems, or taboos related to them, you could be rightly accused of merely paying lip service to the process. You must look carefully at the cultural shift you are making and direct your actions accordingly. People are quick to pick up these cues for success in organizational cultures; if they feel that innovating through power partnering is appreciated, rewarded, and encouraged, then there will be an effort to make it work. This general desire needs to be strengthened by training and by specific programs that provide a framework for power-partnering behavior. Ideally, power partnering should be spread throughout an organization, involving people at all levels and in all areas.

DEVELOPING CAPABILITY

No matter how bold your aspirations and how committed people feel to participating in their attainment, you will do nothing without capability. The best of intentions can only partially make up for a lack of skill, knowledge, and expertise. Developing this expertise is not just a matter of training. I am continuously amazed at how little impact education and training has in comparison to a natural call for something. So how do we create this natural call? How do we make learning meaningful?

Any development and learning strategy should include a combination of learner-centered and expert-centered training methods. While each has its own merits when applied individually, a stagile approach, using both methods, is the only way to make learning meaningful and relevant. This strategic approach to learning emphasizes action and improvement. It encourages immediate, direct, and real learning that serves both individual and organizational requirements and leads to capability in action and creativity in thinking and learning.

Taking a strategic approach to developing capability in power partnering seems like a reasonable way to go because you are applying power-partnering principles to learning. This provides an entirely new way of thinking about knowledge and the way we learn. With its emphasis on action and innovation, within an environment in which immediate, direct, and real learning is encouraged, strategic learning has the dual advantage of serving both individual and organizational requirements and leads to capability in action and creativity in thinking. When you use strategic learning to develop capability, you combine learning with the actual running of your business. Strategic learning develops the knowledge, understanding, will, and spirit of people because learning and sharing knowledge are a natural and permanent aspect of running your enterprise.

Central to the strategic learning approach is the learning commitment, the means by which individual and organizational goals are continually aligned. It is essential that the learning commitment be stagile, reflecting a level of stability that enables people to pursue a path of learning while being sufficiently agile to ensure that their learning remains within the context of your company's aspirations and business strategy.

The learning commitment is created through dialogue among a community of co-learners and other interested people. For example, you may wish to involve your manager, the vice president of human resource development, and the vice president of power partnering and innovation. The importance of this community is that it supports the learning aspirations of its members. The learning commitment is based on the following questions:

1. *Where have I been?* What is my background and previous experience?
2. *Where am I now?* What are the unique capabilities that have allowed me to fulfill my potential so far? What capacity do I have to learn or to develop?
3. *Where am I going?* What are my aspirations, and which abilities will help me fulfill them?
4. *How will I get there?* What development and learning processes and systems will help me acquire the knowledge and understanding I require? How much time can I spare? How much time do I have? How long should I take?
5. *How will I know I have arrived?* What new actions will characterize my success?

Questions 1 and 2 help define capability requirements, while question 3 helps set goals to satisfy those requirements. Question 4 lays out the plan of action, and question 5 provides the basis for assessing completion.

For example, one of my clients decided to shift from being a product-driven to a market-led service business. The owner and his management team knew from the outset that simply imploring people to shift perspectives would not ensure success.

They realized that, to be successful, they had to engage the will and spirit of everyone in the company, as well as develop an entirely new set of abilities. They took a strategic learning approach because they already had excellent teaming skills and a highly interactive organizational design; they wanted a development and learning process that utilized these strengths.

They adopted the following five-stage strategic learning process:

1. They began with some serious listening. They benchmarked market-led service businesses to understand the capability they would require to exceed best-in-class. They held a joint conference with their customers, suppliers, and their customers' customers to understand their aspirations and their expectations of the company. By listening in this way, they were able to create a development and learning strategy that addressed the delta between their current capabilities and their future aspirations.

2. Six-person strategic learning partnerships were set up comprising people from different parts of the organization. These partnerships shared information and developed a map of the critical information and development/learning resources they would need to begin the process of raising awareness.

3. Based on a clear understanding and valuing of the company's aspirations, each strategic learning partnership member wrote a learning commitment outlining her or his objectives, their criteria for success, and the alignment of their learning commitment with the aspirations and strategic plans of the company.

4. People were selected to undergo development as mentors and coaches to assist the strategic learning partnerships and individual members as they put their plans into action.

5. Periodic progress reviews were carried out in conferences with customers, partners, and suppliers to ensure that the development and learning strategy and business aspirations remained aligned.

The breakthrough in this process came from the strategic learning partnerships themselves; the listening process led to the discovery that direct marketing had to be a critical part of their strategy. Consequently, they felt that all members of the company needed a working knowledge of the key concepts and strategy being pursued by the marketing department. This became incorporated into individual learning commitments that strengthened the company's ability to meet its aspirations.

Epilogue

Throughout Western history there has been a pattern of events occurring, every few hundred years or so, that have had a profound effect upon civilization. These events do not happen by accident, but are the cumulative effect of changes in the unconscious thinking of many thousands of people during the period immediately preceding the change. Then, in a relatively short space of time, civilization undergoes a transformational shift in its world view that creates shock waves felt in every walk of society. With dizzying speed, the very fabric of our society changes to such an extent that, less than a generation later, a new world exists and the people born into that world cannot even imagine what life was like in the days of their grandparents and the childhood of their parents.

We are presently undergoing such a transformation. We are living in the midst of accelerating social and economic change and unceasing technological innovation. The lightning-fast demands of our stormy and unforgiving environment are producing overwhelming levels of complexity and ambiguity in our lives. Contemporary organizational practices are failing to respond to this new world order because they are based on outdated assumptions about the way the world works. These tenets, which emphasize power over and control of people, have outlived their usefulness.

My purpose in writing this book has been to offer power partnering as a powerful new framework for seeing and taking advantage of opportunities for innovating in a world of uncertainty and constant change. Power partnering shifts the focus away from analyzing and predicting to designing and innovating where outstanding results are achieved through valuing and openness, sharing information, clustering capabilities, and focusing on teaming those capabilities through creative leadership. It is founded on the belief that every recognizable entity on every scale of existence participates in the universal exchange of energies, supporting and being supported by the existence of others. Said more broadly, the central premise of power partnering is that the fundamental nature of the universe is one of balance and harmony in relationship.

The book provides both a theoretical foundation for power partnering, a framework for setting up power partnerships, and practical suggestions for those wishing to transform their organizations into power-partnering-enterprises. It has been designed to show you ways of applying knowledge in entirely new and innovative ways. Through the practice of power partnering, you will come to regard people who share your aspirations as an important source of learning. Just as churches and monasteries were the source of learning in the agricultural age and businesses the source of learning in the industrial age, in the age of knowledge our source of learning will be those people with whom we choose to establish power partnerships. Whether they be co-workers, suppliers, partners, customers, customers' customers, or combinations of these, your source of knowledge and learning will be the result of the quality of those relationships.

Power partnering uses reverse logic, an alternative to clock logic, to make sense of the world. Reverse logic is based on the belief that we are more than our physical bodies, and that, somewhere within ourselves, lies a source of wisdom and compassion greater than we have known before. Our material, Western-industrialized, clock-logic culture brought us to where we are; but it is no longer sufficient to carry us further without something more. This need for more, this need for wholeness, propels us into the realms of the unconscious mind. For it is here that perceptions are formed and where they stabilize into powerful belief systems. It is here that we must go to discover their true origins, and it is here that we must exercise constant vigilance when we use these beliefs to understand and explain the variety of contexts in which we find ourselves.

If we are to make sense of our increasingly complex world, we must develop mastery in understanding, valuing, and making choices about our own perceptions—and, in so doing, create situations where others might do the same. It is through our perceptions, and the belief systems they form, that we bring meaning and significance into our lives. Our beliefs tell us what things are and what they should be, how things work and how they should work, and why things do what they do. Their presence is so powerful and important to us that we are not always able to grasp the strong truth of our belief systems and how our perceptions know no other truth.

Power-partnering cultures enable creativity. They are built upon a strong foundation of valuing and trust, upon which people interact with one another and their environment in mutually dependent ways. They have shaken themselves free from the legacy of clock logic to acknowledge that their environment is both determined by them and created by them—and that predictability and control are mere illusions. When we attempt to control and predict outcomes, as in the Royal Opera House example, there is little chance to seek out the patterns in events as they unfold and to overlap our talents in order to overcome challenges.

Through building cultures of valuing, it is possible to achieve much more of what we imagine we can do individually. This doesn't mean we abandon all skepticism; as long as we are dealing with different perspectives, different values, and the unpredictability of human behavior, we will always be dealing with misunderstanding. The measure of an effective power-partnering relationship is the extent to which it can encourage intellectual, emotional and spiritual growth, and personal insight through a deeper understanding of, and tolerance for, the perspectives of others.

Power partnerships are founded on principles of valuing whereby we accept, as a basic fact, that we live in separate realities. These principles lead us to the view that if we can see those differing realities as the most promising resource for learning in all the history of the world, if we can live together in order to learn from one another without fear—if we can do all this—then a new age will dawn. Power partnerships are paving the way for just such a change.

Bibliography

Bateson, G. *Steps to an Ecology of Mind*. San Francisco, Calif.: Chandler. [[au: date?]]

Bennett, J.R. *The Dramatic Universe*. 3 vols. Charlestown, West Virginia: Claymont Communications, 1967.

Berry, D. "A Sense of Community." *Transformation* (publication of Gemini Consulting), Issue 3 (Summer 1994).

Blake, A.G.E. *A Seminar on Time*. Charlestown, West Virginia: Claymont Communications, 1980.

Brown, J.S. *HBR* 91101, 1991.

Chopra, D. *The Seven Spiritual Laws of Success*. San Rafael, Calif.: Amber-Allen Publishing/New World Library, 1994.

Clancey, T. *The Hunt for Red October*. Annapolis, Maryland: Naval Institute Press, 1984.

Covey, S. *The Seven Habits of Highly Effective People: Powerful Lessons in Personal Change*. New York: Simon and Schuster, 1989.

De Bono, E. *I Am Right, You are Wrong: From This to the New Renaissance*. London: Penguin Books, 1990.

Dewey, J. *The Quest for Certainty*. New York: Minton, Balch, 1929.

Doane, R. "Sensational Freedoms at Work: Industrial Revolutions." *Inc.*, vol. 4., no. 7 (July 1995).

Erikson, E. *Childhood and Society*. New York: 1963.

Fisher, R. and Ury, W. *Getting to Yes: Negotiating Agreement Without Giving In*. New York: Penguin Books USA Inc, 1983.

Flemons, D.G. *Completing Distinctions: Interweaving the Ideas of Gregory Bateson and Taoism into a Unique Approach to Therapy*. Boston; Shambhala Publications, Inc., 1991.

Gleick, J. *Genius: The Life and Times of Richard Feynman*. New York: Pantheon Books, 1992.

Flores, F. and Winograd, T. *Understanding Computers and Cognition*. Reading, Mass.: Addison-Wesley Publishing Company, Inc., 1987.

Hoff, B. *The Tao of Pooh*. Middlesex: Penguin Books, 1982.

Kane, K.A. "Vision for All to See." *Fast Company* magazine, April-May 1996.

Kelly, G. *The Psychology of Personal Constructs*. New York: Norton, 1955.

Kubler-Ross, E. *On Death and Dying*. London: Tavistock, 1970.

Manville, B. and Foote, N. "Strategy as if Knowledge Mattered." *Fast Company* magazine, April-May 1996.

Maturana, H.R. and Varela, F.J. *The Tree of Knowledge: The Biological Roots of Human Understanding*. Boston: Shambhala Publications, Inc., 1987.

Mintzberg, H. *The Fall and Rise of Strategic Planning*. HBR 94107, 1994.

Morgan, G. *Imaginization: The Art of Creative Management*. London: Sage Publications, 1993.

Morgan, G. and Smircich, L. "Leadership—-The Management of Meaning." *Journal of Applied Behavioral Science*, vol. 18, no. 3 (1982).

O'Brian, T. "Encourage Wild Ideas." *Fast Company* magazine, April-May 1996.

Rogers, C. *A Way of Being*. Boston: Houghton Mifflin Company, 1980.

Savage, C. *Fifth-Generation Management* (revised edition: *Co-creating through Virtual Enterprising, Dynamic Teaming and Knowledge Networking*). Boston: Butterworth-Heinemann, 1996.

Senge, P. and Kofman, F. *Learning Organizations: Developing Cultures for Tomorrow's Workplace*. Cambridge, Mass.: Productivity Press, 1995.

Sheff, D. *The Playboy Interviews with John Lennon and Yoko Ono*. New York: Playboy Press, 1981.

Toffler, A. and H. *Creating a New Civilization: The Politics of the Third Wave*. Atlanta: Turner Publishing, Inc., 1994.

Whyte, L. *The Universe of Experience*. New York: Harper & Row, 1974.

Ziegler, M., Ziegler, B., and Rosenzweig, P. *The Republic of Tea*. New York: Doubleday, 1992.

Post Script

MEMO

To: The Reader

From: Sean

Date: September 4, 1996

Subject: Final Thoughts (for now) on Power
Partnering

Some time ago, I asked my friend Dean Berry to read and comment on my manuscript. Unfortunately, owing to a long stay in the hospital, he has only recently got around to responding. Dean raises some important points about the difficulties, obstacles and barriers to implementing power partnering cultures and even though the manuscript is well on its way to publication, I decided to include this P.S. in response to some of his concerns. First, here is an extract from Dean's memo:

Dear Sean:

Finally I got around to reading Power Partnering. You write wonderfully clearly and sparsely. I envy that. The prose remains good-natured and sprightly throughout the manuscript and the philosophy well integrated and deft; rather than boring and heavy. You underlie and build your points well. These are real gifts!

I am left though with some musings and puzzles. Let me see if I can give language to them.

- *The title and the product. If you want to reach a business audience ("A Strategy for Business Excellence") the business base case has not been addressed except at a very philosophic level (the knowledge era). Here are the two best sources I know for that: Hamel and Prahalad, Strategic Intent and Core Competence, (HBR) as well as Competing for the Future, HBR Press. They make the strategic case; i.e. leveraging resources, stretch, and alliances. At a more profound level, James Moore outlines the coming nature of ecosystems (cooperating across industry boundaries and creating entirely new systems of producing and delivering new consumer benefits) in a book called The Death of Competition (I think he means the death of competition as a sole or primary value). These new paradigms of management are coming fast and some examples already exist in the computer software and chip manufacturing industries, as well as health care. Both authors*

*make the point about the need for mental
shifts—new behaviors and new values—indeed,
new ways of doing business and conceiving
business systems looked at as opportunities as
opposed to philosophy.*

- *So I would be happier with a title that stresses
  more what the book is actually about. To me, it
  is about new philosophies and mind-sets for
  managing in a new age. It's getting ready more
  than doing it. Jordan Lewis's work is about
  "doing it"—and very good it is; both books.
  Yours is; thinking about it, getting ready,
  designing approaches. It isn't really detailed
  enough or gritty enough to be about
  "implementation." Lewis does that, but
  has no philosophy.*

- *I think a much stronger case can also be made
  for why this stuff is so important, how fast it is
  happening and how difficult it is to do well.
  How much "rivalry" cultures have to change
  to accommodate it—which leads me to the
  next point.*

- *Difficulties, obstacles, and barriers are not
  explored. How does one balance, in a firm's
  culture, rivalry and cooperation, trust and
  confidentiality; retaining bargaining power and
  openness? These are very real and very tough
  issues. We agree that new cultures and contexts
  are going to have to be created. We agree that
  new values and governance systems must be a
  new leader's priorities. And how to start it, how*

to think about it is your mutual territory. So is both/and. But how to link it to the real business system? How can the book be credible and not do it?

If any of these notions resonate (and the publishing process time still allows for it), I would be quite willing to dialogue more with you.

Sean, I think you are at the philosophical core of an important issue that bridges business and a new society. Keep up the great work.

All the best,

Dean

MEMO

To: Dean

cc: The Reader

From: Sean

Date: September 9, 1996

Subject: Power Partnering: The Gritty Issues
of Implementing

I was reading your memo over breakfast this morning when, for no apparent reason, the nutrition facts on the side of the cereal box caught my eye. As I am sure you are aware, they are a bunch of facts and figures about the ingredients and essential nutrients contained within the food inside the box. I looked up the meaning of the word 'nutrition' and discovered that it is: the process of nourishing or being nourished; the means by which living organisms assimilate and use food to promote growth and development. It occurred to me that such a definition could be applied to my book: its purpose being to nourish people with food for thought in sufficient quantity to energize them into action; to develop in them the will to transform their organizations into cultures that achieve outstanding results routinely through valuing, encouraging, promoting, and sustaining growth and development among their people. Within its pages I provide a healthy diet, low in fat and cholesterol free, to help readers understand and gain an appreciation for the elements required to build business environments that routinely innovate. These elements, such as new work methods, competencies, and value creating processes, are intentionally designed to leverage the talents, wisdom, and knowledge of all people in ways that lead to innovative products and services that ensure a company's long term competitive advantage.

However, as you quite rightly say, Dean, understanding and gaining an appreciation for the elements required for managing in a new age is not the same as doing it. While I had not originally intended to explore in great detail the difficulties, obstacles, and barriers to power partnering, I agree that such an omission could lead to speculation on the part of the reader that I am a romantic, merely indulging myself in "flights of fancy" with no real foundation for my claims.

The truth of the matter is that over the years I have helped many companies become power partnering enterprises. Many interesting things happened along the way—some great successes and many failures. There are some fundamental reasons why power partnering hasn't worked, and without doubt the number one "show stopper" is a company's tacit assumption that the world is a hostile place. When this happens, a second assumption comes into play: information is knowledge and knowledge is power. When taken to extremes, these tacit assumptions show up in the very fabric and language of the organization. Form follows function. For instance, I know of one company that has ongoing inter-departmental conflicts between sales and manufacturing. Members of the manufacturing department speak of being at the end of a garbage chute, down which salespeople dump orders and yell abuse if orders aren't met. When you look at the facility from the outside, you see that the two departments reside in separate buildings. The sales building sits at a slightly higher elevation than manufacturing and the two are connected by a glass tube.

Criteria about what information gets shared with whom and how it gets transmitted are the architectural blueprints for your organization. Take an airport, for instance. Look around at the symbols of information flow: the uniforms of the employees, their identity tags, and the push button combination locks on doors. They all say something about who knows what. For security reasons, some information is withheld from all but a select few. In other cases, information is displayed for all to see because it is vital to travelers. Similarly, if you choose to withhold information for reasons of security, status or power, or because you feel your marketplace is a violent jungle where the winners are those who play their cards very close to their chest, your internal processes, structures and systems will mirror the hostility you perceive in your external world. This was graphically portrayed in a recent article in the business section of The Boston Sunday Globe. Entitled, "In fight to link computers, elbows fly," the article reads:

> Executives at Cabletron Systems Inc. recently filmed a pair of Boston-based boxers slugging it out in the ring, one eventually beating the other to a pulp. This pugilistic sales pitch, scheduled to be aired later this month at a trade convention in Atlanta, is designed to show what Cabletron would like to do to its rivals Cisco Systems Inc.
>
> Such ribald symbolism—competitors call it antics—is a frequently used motivation

technique at Rochester, NH-based Cabletron, a large manufacturer of computer networking equipment. After all, executives regularly don army fatigues to entreat their sales force to wage a no-holds-barred battle. But the film could also serve as illustration for the entire computer-networking industry. Always competitive, the market for high-tech networking gear is growing even more fiercely contested thanks in large part to the Internet.

When people ask me about the benefits of power partnering, I immediately want to know why they are interested. Some genuinely see the awesome advantages to be gained from fully utilizing their knowledge assets, while others regard it as a pure act of altruism: a nice thing to do for their people, a trendy fad that will make them look good. For those who aspire to anything less than the former, I suggest other, less radical options. As you say, Dean, the changes required to become a power partnering enterprise are more than cosmetic. They go to the very soul of an enterprise. To the place where core values shape the way business gets done.

The following case study captures the key elements in managing change that will bring an organization to its knees if not taken into account. The case blends information from a number of sources, presented in a way that protects the identity of people involved while giving an accurate view of the central issues. The patterns revealed in this case are by no means unique and I am certain readers will find themselves relating to the characters and situations portrayed here. At the end of the case, I will describe the elements that are essential to Power Partnering and ask some key questions which will help readers decide if they are both willing and able to embark upon the journey.

As always, thanks for your insightful ideas and support.

Sean

CASE STUDY: MALCOR INC.

Malcor is a small but rapidly expanding producer of sophisticated electrical components used in advanced micro-electronic communication systems. Over the past ten years, the company has benefited significantly from the sale of products that, until recently, have encountered limited competition in their marketplace. Times are changing and to ensure continued success, company executives have decided to invest in the development of an entirely new generation of communication products produced by a radically new "state of the art" manufacturing process. Malcor executives know that this process is the key to their success because it will enable them to dramatically reduce the time to market of future products. Time is money and reducing new product cycle times means they will continue to enjoy the financial benefits that go along with, not only being the first in the market, but actually defining it. Time is also running out because already there are signs of a slowdown in sales as competition increases.

While on paper, the new products appear innovative and destined to capture the imagination of future customers, they have yet to be designed for manufacturing. In fact, so far nobody from Malcor's production division has been involved in the initial development activities. To make matters worse, nearly all the company's products are built in the Far East, making communication across such vast distances highly problematical. To add to this complexity, Malcor's manufacturing facilities do not want to be involved in the creative process. Their success depends upon low cost manufacturing operations, and in order to achieve this, they need "turn-key" solutions that work the first time. For them, the task of training operators on new machines is about the only cost they are willing to take on.

Company executives appoint Alan Moss to head up the project. Alan has a reputation for, as he puts it, "making things happen." He brings with him an outstanding track record of successful start ups. Soon after his appointment, Alan assembles a team of highly talented design and manufacturing process engineers. Some are hired from within Malcor, but most are from Alan's former company. The team's charter is to create an advanced manufacturing process and associated systems, which will support Malcor's next generation of communication products. Ironically, for a company that makes such products, their own ability to communicate is greatly lacking. While Alan has a clear sense of charter and mission, he sees no benefit in communicating to anyone other than the colleagues be brought in from the outside. The team develops criteria that the new process must satisfy. Criteria such as cost, product performance, and time to market all weigh heavily on their ultimate decision to use an advanced technology known as Micron, a relatively unknown technology first used in military and aerospace applications because of its high reliability in space craft and rocket assisted weapons. While Micron technology has been successfully applied to audio and video consumer products, especially those manufactured in highly automated Japanese factories, nobody has so far attempted to apply Micron technology to micro-electronic products such as those made by Malcor. Clearly, to be first in the industry will give Malcor an unassailable advantage over their nearest rivals. This is the challenge facing the Micron project team.

The first task undertaken by the team is to figure out how to introduce a radically new technology into an existing traditional business culture. Micron is a totally new approach, not a modification of an already existing process. As such, it must function in harmony with existing processes and systems, not as an adjunct to them. Disciplines required for the successful introduction of Micron begin with the initial design concept and end with the acceptance of the product by the customer. In short, its introduction sends shock waves rippling throughout the entire organizational system, with the effects being felt in every phase of the production design and manufacturing process. Also, because Micron has never been used in the design and production of Malcor's products, there are many unknowns. Equipment designs are evolving, software designs are incomplete, work and job designs and organizational structures are undetermined.

You would think that Alan and his team would want to involve as many key figures from these various areas of the company as soon as possible. But this is not the case. He believes he has at his disposal the "best of the best," a team of engineers who know better than anyone the process of introducing new technology into existing systems. While he is warned that Micron must be implemented in combination with other process technologies such as process control, automation, and computer aided or integrated manufacturing, he believes it is his responsibility to control this and people will do as he tells them. This is a dangerous assumption when, among other things, the technology involves the introduction of chemicals which are potentially harmful if not handled skillfully. Also, unlike its traditional counterpart, Micron's complexity makes the inspection and reworking of products extremely difficult and costly. This all requires a radical change in mindset, a new way of looking at the way people approach their work, and this must occur throughout the entire organization.

A number of feasibility studies, carried out prior to the decision to invest in the new manufacturing process, warn of the risks involved in not taking the entire technical and social system into consideration as they plan and execute their program. Alan and his team simply choose to ignore these warnings, an oversight they will live to regret.

Once underway, the project takes on a life of its own. Small teams are formed with little or no awareness of the overall mission of the project. They do as they are told, undertaking a multitude of complex tasks emanating from the project team. Early conversations focus on equipment implementation, tooling, documentation, equipment evaluation, product specification, and people capability. The team's main challenge is to look out three years in time and predict, with a great degree of accuracy, what the process and its accompanying systems might look like. Another challenge is to create a vision of a manufacturing process that is capable of handling high volumes of components, yet be sufficiently modular in design to accommodate new technologies as they emerge. Being self proclaimed experts, team members become engrossed in "crystal ball gazing," seeing no reason to seek the advice from a multitude of sources in order to make the picture clearer. They continually revisit and modify the original plans where necessary, but fail to communicate these to the sub-teams.

This failure to communicate quickly leads to a mood of distrust and lack of commitment among team members and quickly spreads throughout the entire project. Sub-team members blame the senior team members who, in turn, blame Alan, who blames senior management. Everyone feels that they alone, are the only ones "sticking their necks out." They believe that if the project proves successful, management will reap the glory; if it fails, they will deny all knowledge of it.

What nobody realizes is that, behind closed doors, executives at Malcor are embroiled in serious conflicts concerning the funding and approach to be taken in implementing Micron technology. Some want the project to be centrally funded and for the process to become the standard for all future products, while others prefer a more collaborative approach supporting the development of Malcor's next new product, which is scheduled for release in twelve month's time. Executives feel that it is better to apply funding to a known product than to future products that have yet to be designed. After all, resources and funding are already allocated to the project and ready to go. They believe the learning gained from the trial and error of this project will be invaluable to future efforts. As one engineer says, "We can't possibly fail. Even if we have to put the suckers on with tweezers and a magnifying glass, we will be successful because we have a real product to deliver. Every time a problem occurs we know we always have backing. All you have to do is call the right people."

With passions running high, a rift occurs between the executives who desire the prestige of being the first to invent a process that will literally redefine the way products are manufactured for an entire industry and those who prefer a more cautious approach which meets very specific product deadlines and allows learning to take place which can be applied to future products. Unable to reach a compromise, corporate research and development executives give Alan's standard Micron project the O.K., while business unit executives launch their own project intended to develop an advanced manufacturing process for their next new product. From the outset, the stage is set for rivalry and conflict as both teams fight over scarce resources. To compound the issue, corporate research and development are pursuing an entirely different version of Micron, which means that there can be limited sharing of information or pooling of resources because each approach requires entirely different sets of skills.

The conflict is felt at every level of the project, with neither team willing to share information or network their knowledge with the other. They opt instead to pit themselves in mortal combat, where there can only be one winner. Unknown to Alan, the product focus and delivery deadlines of the other project gives it a level of urgency and focus that motivates all those involved. They realize that without collaboration they will fail. The truth is that there is no battle to be fought, the level of support and resources made available to his opponents are way beyond anything Alan can summon up. It's as if his sponsors have gone to sleep on him. Purchase orders take longer and longer to be approved, and as corporate executives move on and new ones take over, his project becomes increasingly less important.

Rather than calling a halt to his project and offering to redirect his resources to the product focused project, Alan and his team simply refuse to accept defeat. As one team member said later, "In some games competition can be fun, especially when each side is on a level playing field, but when the deck is stacked so heavily to one side and when the stakes are so high, such an approach borders on insanity." Unfortunately, insanity prevails and competition is instilled among some very scarce resources. For those people required to support both projects, the task of gathering accurate information is constantly frustrated by misinformation being put out by both teams. As one engineer puts it, "Nobody actually lies to me, but I get partial answers to my questions. I find the same when I ask questions of the other project. If I persist too much, I am told to go away and not to bother people."

As competition increases, Alan begins to hold project meetings at his home to maintain secrecy. As he puts it, "Everyone is making things hard for us, so we will keep things vague enough to throw people off the scent." People become fearful that two rival teams competing for scarce resources will cancel each other out and neither will be successful. Failure will prove costly not only in terms of dollars spent, but more importantly, it will severely damage Malcor's pre-eminent position as a technology leader and prevent it from enjoying the rewards of limited competition. Efforts to stop the conflict are met with denial that any such thing exists. Any hint of rivalry is being blamed on the other team. As one engineer says, "There was no way to blow the whistle in a culture that doesn't recognize the folly of instilling competition among scarce resources. They simply don't see the cost of sustaining two major projects when one collaborative effort is enough."

Ironically, conflicts of this nature are not uncommon at Malcor. In fact, its founder and president, James Malcor, firmly believes in the process of natural selection when it comes to deciding which research and development projects to fund. "May the best man win" is his motto. In the early days, it was not uncommon for several rival projects to be running at the same time and for one to ultimately be selected. While this may have worked 15 years ago, it is clearly inappropriate by today's standards. With less money available and fewer skilled people on the payroll, Malcor simply cannot afford to squander its intellectual and financial capital and hope to stay ahead of the increasing number of competitors in its marketplace.

Frustrated by the conflict, Alan quits Malcor and takes his old colleagues with him. They are replaced by people who are simply not of the same caliber. Not only are they lacking in technical capability but they are totally unable to deal with the political intrigue surrounding the project. To make matters worse, Alan's leaving sends a signal of no confidence to managers, who begin pulling their best people off the project, replacing them with less experienced people. The team's early advantages in technical strength and motivation slowly wane, and as deadlines are missed and expenses climb way beyond projections, the inevitable decision to "pull the plug" on the project is made.

While the second project continues on schedule and within budget, a problem occurs with their advanced Micron process which threatens the entire enterprise. Thankfully, the engineers from Alan's old team are able to help and a major disaster is narrowly avoided. The product is released on time and well within budget. Quality and reliability are outstanding and all indications are that Malcor has, once again, produced a winner. If only people really knew how close they came to disaster.

Lessons from Malcor Inc.

The patterns or themes emerging in this case are by no means unusual and show up time and again in organizations that don't take a power partnering approach to introducing anything new into an established culture. I see the exact same patterns occurring in just about every realm of society, from education, religion, healthcare, and politics, to government and business. They exist in companies as small as ten people and as large as ten thousand. With few exceptions these deep patterns are the result of our natural need for control and predictability, an overwhelming urge to hold things together lest they fall apart.

Although few of us are willing to admit it, major disturbances in the normal flow of our lives are not always welcome. When our world comes crashing down around our ears, we rarely rejoice at the opportunity to learn something new from our challenge. Yet the truth of the matter is that learning and transformation come from such challenges. As self-referencing, self-organizing systems, we are all, to some extent, invested in making our lives predictable and controlled. We are not resistant to change as much as to being changed, and this is the great value of power partnering: its ability to enable people to take ownership and control of the change process. Clearly, Malcor is a culture that deals with complexity by breaking things into little boxes and appointing people to control the boxes. As such, suggestions to overlap and, in some cases, remove boxes and the people that control them will be met with a certain amount of resistance.

How much will depend upon Malcor's willingness to open up to new possibilities and the ability of its people to unite the will and spirit of those who will lead and manage the change process. In Malcor's case, resistance was born out of a lack of unity among some pretty powerful people, and this led to distrust and a searching for weaknesses and faults in other people. Someone had to win, which meant that someone else had to lose. In essence, when Alan's experts attempted to rigidly control things, they excluded the very people who could have helped them. This structured distrust impeded good communication. It blinded people to opportunities. It burdened their efforts. It added unbelievable stress to their work and brittleness to their teams. It added unnecessary costs to their product launch and made them less competitive.

A power partnering approach requires an entirely new mindset about communicating information, generating knowledge, and influencing people. Malcor placed a heavy emphasis on expertise, valuing technical competency over more collaborative mind sharing approaches. To them, people were expected to perform their assigned roles and no more. They were rewarded for services rendered within that role, not for the number of times they stepped out of their box to network their knowledge with others. In fact, the degree to which they did anything innovative was circumscribed by the status their position afforded them, and this was directly linked to the rewards they enjoyed.

From a power partnering perspective, learning, whether personal or organizational, is not regarded as a way of developing the ability to perform certain routines within pre-defined limits, but as a process within life and within whatever we are doing. It is about becoming increasingly perceptive about the patterns that connect us with others and our world. It requires a deep understanding of our feelings and core values and a belief that we have a choice about the direction of our lives. It is a journey along a path which broadens and deepens our understanding of ourselves and the aspirations and capabilities of others and what they cause to happen in the world. Power partnering depends upon our capacity to be willful about our learning and mindful about what is happening around and within us. Fulfilling our potential is a lifelong process of learning from our attempts to fill the voids created when our aspirations exceed our abilities. Power partnering promotes learning through exchanging the lenses through which we view and make sense of our world and with our new lenses open up to new possibilities which come into view.

Introducing power partnering into your company requires a general acceptance that there are voids to be filled and improvements to be made in the value of things. From this perspective, power partnering involves you in a continual and purposeful process of discovering insights, producing action, observing the consequences, and adapting behavior. It is not just about taking in information, but increasing knowledge and deepening understanding about improving action. It emphasizes continuous learning teaming and redefining structure to take advantage of ever changing opportunities. It allows you to provide excellent products and services routinely, while remaining sufficiently agile to seize the rich patterns of possibility that exist in your world.

IF POWER PARTNERING IS THE ANSWER, WHAT WAS THE QUESTION?

The following statements are designed to help you gain an appreciation for your organization's willingness and ability to thrive on complexity. As you respond to each statement, think about the essential qualities required for successful power partnering and decide if they are relevant to you. There are four key themes or patterns that characterize your organization and to a large extend determine how you go about your working, learning, and innovating. Within each pattern there are dimensions arranged as polar opposite statements. For instance, the statement "we have a clear grasp of our potential" is placed in direct contrast to the statement "we have no idea what our potential really is."

The two opposites are linked along a continuum and you should place a mark on the continuum closest to the statement that best describes your position. At the end of the exercise, please enter your overall ratings.

Where We Are Today

OUR POTENTIAL

We consider the exploration and expression of our true potential to be the biggest challenge in our organization.

We constantly seek challenges that bring out the best in us.	We have no idea what we are really capable of, nor do we care.

We organize in ways that bring out the best in people.	We give little thought to the way our organizing brings out the worst in people.

Everything we do is aimed at moving us beyond our perceived limitations.	Everything we do is aimed aimed at maintaining our performance within pre-defined limits.

Our overall rating is:

Optimizing Potential   Constraining Potential

Examples:

OUR PERCEPTION OF TIME

Time is both our enemy and our friend, we must value its ability to focus our attention while not allowing ourselves to become overwhelmed by its scarcity.

Time and timing are critical to our success.	Time and timing are not critical to our success.

●━━━━━━━━━━━━━━━━━━━━━━━━━━●

We organize and coordinate our actions in ways that make the best use of the time we have.	We organize and coordinate our actions based on status and privileged access to information.

●━━━━━━━━━━━━━━━━━━━━━━━━━━●

Time is our friend. Without it we would not feel challenged to meet our commitments in a timely manner.	Time is our enemy. It limits the amount we feel we can commit to people. If only we had more time, life would be different

●━━━━━━━━━━━━━━━━━━━━━━━━━━●

Our overall rating is:

Optimizing Time	Constraining Time

●━━━━━━━━━━━━━━━━━━━━━━━━━━●

Examples:

OUR CAPABILITY

As we take on the challenges in our environment we constantly maintain alignment between our aspirations and our capabilities.

Our intellectual capability is the key to our success.	Our financial capability is the key to our success.

●━━━━━━━━━━━━━━━━━━━━━━━━━━━━●

We build on and leverage the talents and capabilities of all our people.	We hire in talent when we need it and send people to training courses if their performance drops below par.

●━━━━━━━━━━━━━━━━━━━━━━━━━━━━●

Our intellectual assets are of greater value to us than our financial assets.	Our financial assets are of greater value to us than our intellectual assets.

●━━━━━━━━━━━━━━━━━━━━━━━━━━━━●

Our overall rating is:

Optimizing Capability	Constraining Capability

●━━━━━━━━━━━━━━━━━━━━━━━━━━━━●

Examples:

BUSINESS ENVIRONMENT

We constantly gather information about our environment that allows us to understand our relative position and the rich patterns of possibility out there.

We continually seek out the possibilities in our environment.	We look for a market opportunity and stick with it.

●━━━━━━━━━━━━━━━━━━━━━━━━━━━●

We constantly re-invent ourselves through providing innovative products and services that delight our customers.	We stick to the knitting and only respond to changes in our industry when trends indicate we must.

●━━━━━━━━━━━━━━━━━━━━━━━━━━━●

Routine innovation is our key to success and longevity.	Sticking to the knitting is our key to success and longevity.

●━━━━━━━━━━━━━━━━━━━━━━━━━━━●

Our overall rating is:

Optimizing our environment	Constraining our environment

●━━━━━━━━━━━━━━━━━━━━━━━━━━━●

Examples:

ALIGNING WHAT WE DO WITH WHO WE ARE

We carry out our work to the highest ethical and moral standards. We continually question our espoused values and align our actions accordingly.

We know the essential qualities that cause us to be who we are.	We give little thought to who we really are.

We know the essential qualities that cause us to do what we do.

We care little about the thinking behind our actions.

Our overall rating is:

Optimizing our essence.

Constraining our essence.

Examples:

Where We Want to Be

Now think about a major challenge you wish to undertake. The following statements are designed to help you assess your willingness to relentlessly pursue your aspirations in the face of adversity and complexity and see the process through to the end. Once again, as you review each statement, think about the relevance power partnering might have to your cause. In the second part of this exercise there are four key themes or patterns, each characterizing an aspect of your organization's will to attain that which is aspires to become. Each theme has a statement describing how your organization might value each. To score this section place a low, medium, or high mark in the appropriate place. At the end of the exercise, please enter your overall ratings:

NEW POSSIBILITIES

We continually monitor the gap between our potential, our capabilities and the time we have at our disposal.

Low   Medium   High

We regard the gap between our potential and our capabilities as opportunities to learn and continually improve our performance.

Low   Medium   High

ASPIRATIONS AND VALUES

We have a clear appreciation for the capabilities required to ensure success.

Low   Medium   High

We fully understand the changing circumstances we will encounter on our journey and the capabilities we will require to meet them.

Low   Medium   High

We have clear and agreed organizational aspirations and operating principles and use these to guide our actions and ensure we have the right capabilities in place at the right time.

Low   Medium   High

STRUCTURE

We are aware of the voids existing in our environment that offer outstanding possibility.

●————————————————————————————————●

Low   Medium   High

We understand the factors that determine the amount of time available to pursue these possibilities.

●————————————————————————————————●

Low   Medium   High

Our organization's processes, systems and structures are specifically designed to optimize space and time and provide excellent coordination of minds and action.

●————————————————————————————————●

Low   Medium   High

CAUSE

All members of our organization understand and buy into our core mission.

Low   Medium   High

Given the many possibilities we identify in our environment, we accept our limitations while not allowing them to constrain our ability to achieve great things. When the dust looks like its beginning to settle we shake it up again.

Low   Medium   High

We are clear on the cause we intend to uphold to effectively relate our organization's potential with the challenges in our environment.

Low   Medium   High

SUMMARY SCORES

Where We Are Today

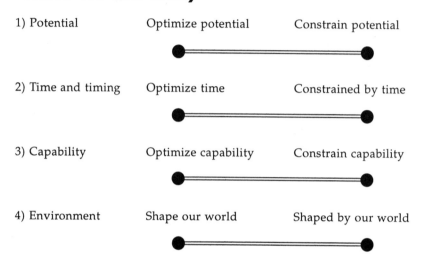

1) Potential   Optimize potential   Constrain potential

2) Time and timing   Optimize time   Constrained by time

3) Capability   Optimize capability   Constrain capability

4) Environment   Shape our world   Shaped by our world

Where We Want to Be

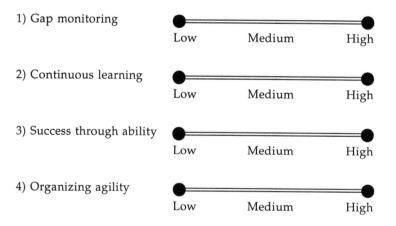

1) Gap monitoring   Low   Medium   High

2) Continuous learning   Low   Medium   High

3) Success through ability   Low   Medium   High

4) Organizing agility   Low   Medium   High

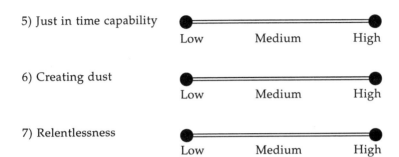

5) Just in time capability

Low   Medium   High

6) Creating dust

Low   Medium   High

7) Relentlessness

Low   Medium   High

CONCLUSION

So what is your score telling you? Are you ready to shrink the time it takes for you to transform innovative ideas into products and services using power partnerships? If you did the exercise as a team, how many skeptics did you have? How many thought "it's a good idea but...."? Unless your scores indicate a strong willingness to adopt a radically new approach to working, learning, and innovating, you should think twice about moving ahead.

Serious change requires serious belief without evidence. The journey is always far worse than the initial conditions that led up to it. When the going gets tough, the uncommitted struggle to restore the status quo, no matter how bad it used to be. Without your committed participation as leaders, there will be no sustained appreciation for the future you aspire to bring about. As leaders, you must maintain unity through a compelling vision kept alive in the mind's eye of people. A focus in common that endures the hazard you encounter along the way. For those who believe power partnering is the way to go, I wish you good fortune.

Index

Dr. Sean Gadman has over 20 years experience in international management and consulting. His clients include Shell International, Canada Life Assurance, Keiser Aluminum and Chemical Corporation, Rio Tinto Zinc, Digital Equipment Corporation, and VHA Healthfront.

Sean is president of Teknowledging, Inc., an international consulting organization helping companies create value for their customers, shareholders, and members through dynamic and proactive knowledge partnering. He is also a principle in Pricetrak, Inc., a provider of IT-based knowledge partnering systems that helps companies optimize the price of products and services through highly creative and innovative purchasing.

Sean consults and leads seminars internationally with company presidents and other executives who are committed to transforming their organizations into power partnering enterprises that create value through fully utilizing their financial and intellectual capital.

Sean earned his Ph.D. in Organizational Behavior from the University of Lancaster in England. He lives in Salisbury, Massachusetts.